Queen Wilhelmina – A collection of articles

2020

Published by Amazon KDP 2020

Copyright © Moniek Bloks / History of Royal Women

ISBN: 9798563117860

Introduction

This collection of articles was written for the History of Royal Women website during the year 2020 to celebrate 140 years since the birth of Queen Wilhelmina of the Netherlands. You'll find that the articles are not listed chronologically by year, but rather by day and month as the events happened over the years.

This collection is in no way meant to be a full biography of Queen Wilhelmina but will hopefully give you a glimpse into her personal life nevertheless. As the articles were initially meant to stand alone, you may find some repetition.

Wilhelmina was an extraordinary woman, born under extraordinary circumstances, shaped by the world she lived in.

Moniek Bloks
History of Royal Women

See also our previous publications:
Carolina of Orange-Nassau: Ancestress of the Royal Houses of Europe (2019)
Hermine: An Empress in Exile: The Untold Story of the Kaiser's Second Wife (2020)

JANUARY

7 January 1879 - The wedding of King William III of the Netherlands and Princess Emma of Waldeck and Pyrmont

Emma and William RP-F-F21080 via Rijksmuseum (public domain)

Wilhelmina would be the only child of the 22-year-old Emma of Waldeck and Pyrmont and the 63-year-old King William III of the Netherlands. They were both descendants of Carolina of Orange-Nassau.

William had been married once before - to his first cousin Sophie of Württemberg - and they had had three sons together. The succession seemed secure, one would think.

However, their second son Maurice died at the age of 6 of meningitis. Their eldest son William and their youngest son Alexander were both still alive when their mother died in 1877 but it seems that King William already realised they would not have children.

The younger William was denied marriage to Countess Mathilde von Limburg-Stirum who was considered too low in rank for a future King. In addition, there were rumours that she could be one of King William's bastard children, making her the younger William's half-sister! He left the Netherlands to settle in Paris, where he lived a debauched lifestyle. Alexander had always been nervous and sickly and he shied away from women.

King William met Emma as he was taking the cure in Pyrmont. He initially came to court her elder sister Pauline who rejected the elderly King but her sister Emma supposed exclaimed, "We cannot just let the poor man go home alone!" Their engagement was announced on 30 September 1878. A tutor was dispatched to teach Emma Dutch, though she would always struggle with spelling and grammar.

The wedding of Emma and King William took place in the chapel of Arolsen on 7 January 1879 when they were 20 and 61 respectively. The groom wore the uniform of an admiral and the bride wore a white dress with a long train, a lace veil, a tiara and an ermine shoulder cover.

The entire Princely family of Waldeck and Pyrmont was there, plus Charles Alexander, Grand Duke of Saxe-Weimar-Eisenach and his wife, Princess Sophie of the Netherlands (William's sister),

William, Prince of Wied (husband of Princess Marie of the Netherlands, granddaughter of King William I), Duke William of Württemberg, Georg, Prince of Schaumburg-Lippe and his wife Princess Marie Anne of Saxe-Altenburg. The Netherlands was represented by the Minister of Foreign Affairs, the presidents of both houses of the States-General and the vice-president of the Council of State. The court preacher Ulrich Scipio blessed the marriage.[1]

Notable absentees were King William's sons who were both shocked by their father's upcoming nuptials. The younger William must have been especially hurt after being denied his Countess and he reportedly ordered the windows of his palace at Kneuterdijk boarded shut in protest.

On 10 January 1879, Emma joined her husband on the journey home to a court where she would not be welcomed with open arms and yet, she managed to charm a nation and provide them with an heir - to which the year 2020 - also the 140th anniversary of Wilhelmina's birth - is dedicated.

---

[1] Het Nederlandse koningshuis by Arnout van Cruyningen p.108

7 January 1937 – The wedding of Princess Juliana and Prince Bernhard of Lippe-Biesterfeld

Portrait of Juliana and Bernhard flanked by their mothers Armgard (l) and Wilhelmina (r)

NG-1980-37-53-B via Rijksmuseum: Legaat van de heer R. van Luttervelt, Lochem (public domain)

On the 58th wedding anniversary of King William III of the Netherlands and Emma of Waldeck and Pyrmont, their only grandchild Princess Juliana - heir to the Dutch throne - married Prince Bernhard of Lippe-Biesterfeld.

Juliana had been born in 1909, and she had long searched for a suitable match. In 1936, she had met Prince Bernhard of Lippe-Biesterfeld, and it is likely that Hermine Reuss of Greiz - the second wife of the exiled German Emperor who lived in The Netherlands - encouraged him and put in a good word for him. He charmed Juliana, and she soon fell in love with him. He visited the Netherlands during Easter and also won the approval of Queen Wilhelmina.

On 8 September 1936, the engagement was announced to the Dutch people. Bernhard became a naturalised citizen and he received several military positions. He was also made a Prince of the Netherlands. He was marrying a future Queen after all.

On 7 January 1937, they were married in a civil ceremony at the city hall in The Hague, followed by a religious service in the Great Church. It was the same church where Queen Wilhelmina had married Duke Henry of Mecklenburg-Schwerin in 1901. On the day of her wedding, Juliana had white arums placed on Henry's grave in Delft. Juliana's dress was meant to look like a robe of a Greek goddess, but it received little praise. It was a white satin dress with a thick flannel lining to protect the bride from the cold.

During the honeymoon, people already noticed Bernhard's cold behaviour towards his new wife, writing, "He may be a Prince, but he is no gentleman."[2]

After a honeymoon lasting three months - to Queen Wilhelmina's horror! - the newlyweds settled into Soestdijk Palace.

---

[2] Juliana by Jolande Withuis p.197

Juliana fell pregnant during the honeymoon and announced her pregnancy herself on the radio on 15 June 1937. A new generation was coming, and Queen Wilhelmina would soon become a grandmother.

19 January 1943 - The life of Princess Margriet

Prince Bernhard with Princess Margriet RP-F-00-7557 via Rijksmuseum (public domain)

After many years of the Dutch succession depending on a single heartbeat, the birth of a healthy third daughter to the heiress presumptive Princess Juliana came as a huge relief.

Princess Juliana was Queen Wilhelmina's only surviving child, and she had given birth to a daughter named Beatrix in 1938 and a daughter named Irene in 1939. She had suffered a miscarriage in 1941.

The circumstances surrounding Margriet's birth were not the happiest. In May 1940 Princess Juliana and her family were evacuated to the United Kingdom at the start of the Second World War. A month later, the family travelled on to Ottawa in Canada, which is where Margriet was born on 19 January 1943. Wilhelmina received a telephone call from her son-in-law Bernhard at half-past one in the morning to inform her of the birth of her third grandchild. She would not meet her new grandchild until several months later when she visited Canada for the christening. The christening took place on 29 June 1943 at the St. Andrews Church in Ottawa. Margriet would not return to Dutch soil until 2 August 1945 after the liberation of the Netherlands. The final years before Queen Wilhelmina's abdication, Margriet and her family lived at Soestdijk Palace where her mother prepared to take over as Queen. A fourth daughter named Maria Christina (Marijke, later known as Christina) was born on 18 February 1947. Juliana had contracted rubella during the pregnancy and Christina was born nearly blind. It weighed heavily on Juliana. On 4 September 1948, Queen Wilhelmina abdicated in her daughter's favour, and Margriet was now the daughter of a Queen. Margriet was sent to the same progressive school as her two elder sisters in 1949. The girls' father was not happy with the school as it did not focus on academic achievements. Margriet continued her studies at the Baarns Lyceum from which she graduated in 1961.

Afterwards, she went to study at the University of Montpellier in

France for a year before applying to study law at the University of Leiden. She also trained with the Red Cross in Amersfoort. During her studies in Leiden, Margriet would meet her future husband, Pieter van Vollenhoven.

Margriet and Pieter's engagement was announced on 10 March 1965, and they were married on 10 January 1967 in The Hague. They moved into The Loo Palace after their wedding before moving to Huis Het Loo, near the palace in 1975. They went on to have four sons together, and their sons were granted the title "Prince of Orange-Nassau" and with "Highness" as a style of address. Their father has remained untitled. They currently also have 11 grandchildren.

Photo by author

Princess Margriet has moved from being the monarch's granddaughter to the monarch's daughter to being the monarch's aunt.

She still performs royal duties for her nephew King Willem-Alexander. She is currently eighth and last in the line of succession. Her sons are not in the line of succession because they are not within three degrees of kinship to the monarch.[3]

---

[3] Website Koninklijk Huis, Juliana & Bernhard by Cees Fasseur and Juliana by Jolande Withuis

23 January 1912 - Wilhelmina's fourth miscarriage

With Wilhelmina's marriage to Henry of Mecklenburg-Schwerin on 7 February 1901, she and her mother both fervently prayed for healthy children to continue their line. Tragically, Wilhelmina would go on to suffer five miscarriages and only one healthy child was born to Wilhelmina and Henry.

At the end of 1911, Queen Wilhelmina was pregnant again, and she was due in August 1912. However, on 23 January 1912 - three years after the birth of Princess Juliana - Queen Wilhelmina suffered her fourth miscarriage.

The New York Times reported: "An official communication today confirms the report that the hopes of the birth of an heir to the throne of the Netherlands[4] has been shattered. The condition of Queen Wilhelmina, who has been indisposed for some days, is now stated by the physicians in attendance to be satisfactory."[5]

Queen Wilhelmina later wrote to her mother-in-law, "It was a difficult time for us in every respect. But God has helped us and given us the strength to get through it."[6]

A fifth and final miscarriage would follow in October 1912 - leaving Juliana as the sole heir to the throne.

---

[4] They mean a male heir

[5] New York Times 23 January 1911

[6] Wilhelmina de jonge Koningin by Cees Fasseur p. 324

31 January 1938 - The life of Princess Beatrix

Juliana and Beatrix RP-F-00-7565 via Rijksmuseum (public domain)

On Monday morning 31 January 1938, Queen Wilhelmina's first grandchild, the future Queen Beatrix, was born at Soestdijk Palace. She was given the names Beatrix Wilhelmina Armgard, for both her grandmothers. She weighed eight pounds and was 52 centimetres long. Her parents were Queen Wilhelmina's only surviving child Princess Juliana and her husband, Prince Bernhard.

She was baptised on 12 May 1938. Her five godparents were King

Leopold III of Belgium, Princess Alice, Countess of Athlone, Elisabeth, Princess of Erbach-Schönberg, Duke Adolf Friedrich of Mecklenburg, and Countess Allene de Kotzebue.

Shortly before the start of the Second World War, she was joined in the nursery by a younger sister named Princess Irene. It soon became clear that the Netherlands would not be able to stay neutral during this war as it had been during the First World War. The night before the invasion, Queen Wilhelmina joined Juliana and her two granddaughters in a bomb shelter near Huis ten Bosch. On 13 May, the family boarded the HMS Hereward and were evacuated to the United Kingdom. Queen Wilhelmina set up a government in exile while Juliana, Beatrix and Irene were sent to Lydney Park in Gloucestershire. Soon there were plans to move them to Canada where they would be safer.

Meanwhile, Princess Irene's baptism took place in the Royal Chapel of Buckingham Palace. On 2 June 1940, Juliana and her two daughters left for Canada on the Sumatra - arriving there on 10 June. Beatrix's father Prince Bernhard remained in England.

In 1942, Queen Wilhelmina visited her family in Ottawa, where she was also joined by President Roosevelt, his wife and Princess Märtha of Sweden, Crown Princess of Norway. Beatrix and Irene stole the show, and Roosevelt's secretary later wrote, "Princess Beatrix gave me some cherries from her basket, and the other little toddler gave me a posy.

"Really adorable children and great favourites with all the men on duty here."[7] Queen Wilhelmina then travelled on to the United States where she would address a joint session of the United States Congress. In early 1943, a third daughter named Margriet was born to Princess Juliana in Canada. The three little Princesses all learned to speak English with a Canadian accent. During their time in Canada, Beatrix attended nursery and Rockcliffe Park Public School, where she was known as "Trixie Orange."

After a visit in August 1945, Queen Mary wrote, "Such talkative children, too funny, the baby (Margriet) climbing all over the furniture... They told us all about the ship Queen Mary... all in broad Canadian English."[8]

On 2 August 1945, the family was finally able to return to the liberated Netherlands. They went to live at Soestdijk Palace, where Beatrix had been born. Beatrix continued her education at De Werkplaats in Bilthoven. A fourth and final daughter - Maria Christina (later just Christina) was born to Princess Julia in 1947, but she suffered from limited eyesight after her mother had become infected with rubella during her pregnancy. More changes were to come when her grandmother Queen Wilhelmina abdicated on 4 September 1948 and Beatrix was now the heir to the throne. Meanwhile, her education went ahead as planned.

In 1950, she went to the Incrementum, part of the Baarns Lyceum, from which she graduated in 1956. She then attended Leiden

---

[7] Wilhelmina - Krijgshaftig in een vormeloze jas by Cees Fasseur p.397

[8] Wilhelmina - Krijgshaftig in een vormeloze jas by Cees Fasseur p.415

University, where she studied Law, and she gained her degree in 1961.

Beatrix's engagement to German diplomat Claus von Amsberg was announced on 28 June 1965 by her mother and father. They were married on 10 March 1966 and despite protests on their wedding day (due to him being German), he eventually became one of the more popular members of the royal family. They had met at the wedding of Princess Tatjana of Sayn-Wittgenstein-Berleburg and Moritz, Landgrave of Hesse. The newlyweds went to live at Drakensteyn Castle, and they went on to have three sons together: the current King Willem-Alexander (1967), Prince Friso (1968–2013) and Prince Constantijn (1969). They lived at Drakensteyn Castle until the abdication of Beatrix's mother Juliana in 1980 when they moved to Huis ten Bosch.

On 30 April 1980, Beatrix became Queen of the Netherlands when her mother abdicated in her favour. She was inaugurated at a ceremony held in the Nieuwe Kerk in Amsterdam later that day. She would go on to reign as Queen for 33 years. Tragically, she lost her husband in 2002 after a long illness. Both her father and mother followed in 2004. She celebrated her silver jubilee in 2005 and received an honorary doctorate from the Leiden University that same year.

On Queen's Day - the traditional birthday celebrations of the monarch - in 2009, there was an attack on the bus that the royal family were riding in. A man in a car crashed through a crowd of people - killing 8 (including the attacker) - but he missed the bus and crashed into a monument. The royal family was not hurt but witnessed much of the attack. A visibly emotional Queen Beatrix addressed the nation via live television a few hours later.

On 28 January 2013, Beatrix announced her intention to abdicate and she did so on 30 April 2013 - becoming the third successive monarch to abdicate. Prime Minister Rutte paid tribute to her saying, "Since her investiture in 1980, she has applied herself heart and soul to Dutch society." The inauguration of her son - now King Willem-Alexander - took place in the afternoon on 30 April. Just a few months later, her middle son Prince Friso died of complications after being in a coma following an avalanche accident.

Queen Beatrix reverted to using the title of Princess, and despite abdicating, she is still an active member of the royal family. Through her three sons, she has eight grandchildren.[9]

---

[9] See also her biography on the Koninklijk Huis website

FEBRUARY

7 February 1901 - The wedding of Queen Wilhelmina and Duke Henry of Mecklenburg-Schwerin

The wedding day RP-F-F03162 via Rijksmuseum (public domain)

On 7 February 1901, the young Queen Wilhelmina of the Netherlands married Duke Henry of Mecklenburg-Schwerin. He was one of three candidates who had been considered for the young Queen.

Any British candidates had been vetoed because of the Boer War, and even Emperor Wilhelm II butted in and declared that only a German Prince would do. In May 1900, Wilhelmina and her mother Emma travelled to Schloss Schwarzburg in Thuringia to meet the three possibilities.

They were: Frederick Henry (Friedrich Heinrich) of Prussia, who was a grandson of Princess Marianne of the Netherlands, and the two youngest sons of Frederick Francis II, Grand Duke of Mecklenburg-Schwerin, Adolf and Henry (Heinrich), but Adolf did not show up.

Wilhelmina had met Henry previously in 1892 when she was just 12 years old, and they were second cousins as they were both descended from Paul I of Russia and Maria Feodorovna.

They met several times over the next few months after Wilhelmina had quickly vetoed Frederick Henry. In her memoirs, she wrote of their engagement in October, "On the 12th of October he came to luncheon. After the meal was over, the others withdrew and left us alone. Ten minutes later, we returned and announced our engagement. The die was cast. What a relief that always is on these occasions!"[10] On 29 October, Wilhelmina excitedly wrote to her former governess Miss Winter, "Oh, Darling, you cannot even faintly imagine how frantically happy I am and how much joy and sunshine has come upon my path."[11]

The months leading up to the wedding were wrought with financial arrangements and discussions about the name of the House. Nevertheless, Wilhelmina was thrilled, and she wrote to Miss Winter, "Oh, you don't know how I am longing for my wedding to come to no more be separated from him and be able to live for him, what a happiness!"[12]

---

[10] Lonely but not alone p.98

[11] Darling Queen, Dear Old Bones edited by Emerentia van Heuven-van Nes p.271

[12] Darling Queen, Dear Old Bones edited by Emerentia van Heuven-van Nes p.272

The Great Church in The Hague was chosen as the wedding venue, but celebrations had to be shortened following the deaths of Wilhelmina's uncle the Grand Duke of Saxe-Weimar-Eisenach on 5 January and Queen Victoria on 22 January. On 31 January, Henry arrived in the Netherlands for the wedding. Several events took place over the following days, like a theatre performance and a soiree with tableaux vivants.

The day of the wedding was a sunny but cold day. Crowds had gathered in the streets to catch a glimpse of the bride and groom. The civil wedding was performed at Noordeinde Palace before they were taken to the Great Church in the Golden Carriage. Wilhelmina did not agree to obey her husband. Following the ceremony, there was a breakfast at the Palace. Emma toasted the couple with the words, "In full confidence, I gave my child to the man of her choice."[13] Emma would move into a palace of her own after the wedding - Lange Voorhout Palace. Wilhelmina later wrote, "It was a magnificent wedding. Many members of both families were present, and the whole country rejoiced in our happiness. We received splendid presents, including the golden coach, offered to me by Amsterdam in 1898, which was finished just in time."[14]

They spent their honeymoon at the snow-covered Loo Palace.

---

[13] Wilhelmina - De Jonge Koningin by Cees Fasseur p.249

[14] Lonely but not alone p.64

18 February 1947 - The life of Princess Christina

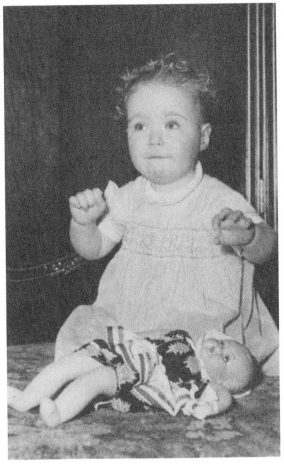

Princess Christina RP-F-00-7593 via Rijksmuseum (public domain)

At the end of August 1946, after the Dutch royal family were all reunited in the Netherlands after the Second World War, a press release announced that Princess Juliana would have to limit her duties due to "happy circumstances." She was pregnant for the fourth time, but she was worried about the pregnancy because she knew she had been infected with rubella.

Rubella can be fatal for a fetus, and if it survives, it can lead to blindness and deafness, among other things. On 18 February 1947, Princess Juliana gave birth to a daughter named Maria Christina (first known as Marijke and then as just Christina). Unfortunately, as Juliana had feared, Christina suffered from blindness in one eye and cataracts in the other eye. The news of her condition was announced a month after her birth. Juliana blamed herself, eventually leading to the introduction of the faith healer Greet Hofmans at court. Just one year later, Christina's grandmother Queen Wilhelmina abdicated the throne in favour of Juliana and she now also had to bear the heavy burden of the crown.

The faith healer would be unable to heal her patient and was later banned from court.

Christina attended the social academy De Horst in Driebergen, and she also took classes at the University of Groningen. In 1968, she moved to Canada to follow singing and music classes at the École de musique Vincent-d'Indy in Montreal. She also attended McGill University. She eventually worked as a vocal pedagogue in New York, where she would meet her future husband - Jorge Guillermo, a Cuban exile. She often sang for her family during official events, such as the funerals of her parents and the wedding of her son Bernardo.

They were civilly married on 28 June 1975 in Baarn, followed by a religious ceremony in Utrecht. Christina chose not to ask for permission from parliament to marry and subsequently forfeited her rights to the throne. They initially lived in New York before moving back to the Netherlands in 1984. They went on to have three children together: Bernardo Federico Tomás (born 17 June 1977), Nicolás Daniel Mauricio (born 6 July 1979) and Juliana Edenia Antonia (born 8 October 1981). They finally settled in Villa Eikenhorst in Wassenaar. In 1992, Christina officially converted to Catholicism. Her marriage to Jorge ended in divorce in 1994, and she settled in New York with her sons while her daughter went to live with her father in London. In New York, Christina was a vocal coach, and she recorded several albums. From 1989, she supported an annual competition held in the Netherlands to encourage musical talent in children, and it was named the Prinses Christina Concours for her. Christina was also a dance therapist who worked with dance and sound therapy with the blind.

In 2018, Princess Christina was diagnosed with bone cancer, and she passed away at Noordeinde Palace on 16 August 2019 at the age of 72. She was the first of Queen Wilhelmina's grandchildren to pass away. For what she had achieved despite her blindness, Christina was Juliana's greatest pride.

She had "made it all on her own" because of her "strong personality."[15]

[15] Juliana by Jolande Withuis p.622

19 February 1817 - The life of King William III of the Netherlands

King William III of the Netherlands RP-F-1994-62-48 via Rijksmuseum (public domain)

The future King William III of the Netherlands was born on 19 February 1817 as the eldest son of the future King William II of the Netherlands and his wife, Anna Pavlovna of Russia.

He was born in Brussels, which was then still part of the Kingdom of the Netherlands.

He was baptised in the Augustine Church in Brussels on 27 March 1817 with the names William Alexander Paul Frederick Louis. Four more siblings would later join the nursery: Prince Alexander (1818 - 1848), Prince Henry (1820 - 1879), Prince Ernest Casimir (1822 - 1822) and Princess Sophie (1824 – 1897). He spent his early years mostly in Brussels as it was the preferred residence of his parents. The education of the boys was entrusted to Thierry Juste baron de Constant Rebecque de Villars - a soldier. It was an intense schedule of studying - six days a week.

William was 13 years old when Belgium became a separate Kingdom, and he saw his future Kingdom being cut in half. In 1836, William, Alexander and their parents visited England where William danced with the future Queen Victoria. By then, he had already begun his studies at the University of Leiden, which he completed in 1837. He had not spent much time in class and instead received tutoring at home.

On 18 June 1839, William married his first wife Sophie of Württemberg, who was also his first cousin. They were married in Stuttgart, and the return journey to the Netherlands also served as their honeymoon. They took their time returning and did not cross the Dutch border at Arnhem until a month later. Sophie and her mother-in-law and aunt Anna did not get along at all, and she had not approved of him marrying her. William and Sophie were not a match made in heaven.

She considered him childish and less intelligent than her. He had no moral compass and often had fits of rage.

Nevertheless, Sophie fulfilled her duty and gave birth to her first son on 4 September 1840. It was to be yet another William, though he would be known as Wiwill in the family. Just one month after young William's birth, King William I abdicated the throne in order to marry his late wife's lady-in-waiting, Henriette d'Oultremont. William's father now became King William II of the Netherlands, and William became Prince of Orange as the heir to the throne. On 15 September 1843, a second son named Maurice was born to them. Their marriage remained unhappy, and Sophie even confided in her sister-in-law that she had asked God to let her die in childbirth. William raged against her and also physically attacked her. She did not think William was fit to be King and feared the day, "the King would close his eyes forever. I am begging God on my knees that it may last quite a while yet."

Unfortunately, the day would come sooner than expected. On 17 March 1849, King William II died in his newly-built palace in Tilburg after a short illness. His son, who was in England at the time, did not learn of his death until a day later. William had already shown himself to be reluctant to become King, especially after the new Constitution of 1848 limited the monarch's powers even more. As he slowly travelled back to the Netherlands, he continued to doubt if he would accept the crown and had to be persuaded to do so. On 12 May 1849, his inauguration took place in the New Church in Amsterdam.

Even Sophie was impressed and later wrote, "My King behaved himself exceptionally and spoke clearly and with dignity. All and all, we have made a good impression."

However, tragedy was to come. In May 1850, young Maurice fell ill with meningitis. He died on 4 June 1850 and Sophie never forgave herself for calling on a new doctor. Their shared grief did bring the couple closer together for a time, and Sophie gave birth to a third son named Prince Alexander on 25 August 1851. But their relationship never quite healed and William found solace elsewhere. Sophie even began a divorce proceeding against her husband, but on her father's advice, she eventually decided not to proceed. They lived separate lives as much as they could. In the end, their marriage would last until Sophie's death, which took place on 3 June 1877.

Sophie and William's eldest son was at his mother's funeral in Delft, but it was a rare sighting of the Prince of Orange in the Netherlands. He spent most of his time in Paris, where he lived a debauched lifestyle. He had been denied marriage to Mathilde, Countess of Limburg-Stirum. His younger brother Alexander was considered to be "weak" and unlikely to marry and father children. This left William's brother Prince Henry as a possible heir, but he was a widower (his first wife was Amalia of Saxe-Weimar-Eisenach) and childless. A second marriage to Marie of Prussia in 1878 ended with Henry's death just five months later. Another possible heir was William's elderly uncle Frederick, who had two daughters (Louise and Marie).

The most likely scenario seemed to be that if William's son did not have any offspring that the non-ruling descendants of his sister Sophie would take the throne (the Dutch crown could not be united with a foreign crown). William did not want to see a "stranger" on the Dutch throne. Young William's debauched lifestyle caught up with him, and he died on 11 June 1879.

By then, William had decided to clear up the succession issues himself. He would marry again. His first instinct had been to marry his mistress, but the following public outrage changed his mind. European Princesses were now being lined up for the elderly King. His first choice was Princess Thyra of Denmark, daughter of King Christian IX, who tactfully informed William that his daughter "did not feel capable of fulfilling such a serious and difficult task." He then approached Princess Marie of Hanover, daughter of King George V of Hanover, and her father refused to consent to the match on his deathbed. He then contacted his sister Sophie, whose daughter Elisabeth was of marriageable age. He personally travelled to Weimar, but Elisabeth felt such a "deep aversion" for her elderly uncle that she could not bring herself to agree to a match.

William then continued his travels to Pyrmont where he was picked up at the train station by George Victor, Prince of Waldeck and Pyrmont. His three daughters also happened to be there: Pauline, Emma and Marie. Marie had married in 1877, but Pauline and Emma were still available. William initially only had eyes for the eldest sister Pauline, but she thought he was too old for her. His attention then shifted to Emma. He stayed for four days before returning home with a spring in his step. Emma had caught his eye. On 7 January 1879, the 61-year-old William married the 20-year-old Emma at Arolsen. The groom wore the uniform of an admiral, and the bride wore a white dress with a long train, a lace veil, a tiara and an ermine shoulder cover. Emma would have a good influence on William and in 1882 Queen Victoria wrote to her eldest daughter,

"The King of the Netherlands is as quiet and unobtrusive as possible; a totally altered man and totally owing to her. She is charming, so amiable, kind, friendly and cheerful."

On 15 March 1880, the couple announced happy news; Emma was pregnant. On 31 August 1880, Emma gave birth to a daughter named Wilhelmina. William was delighted with the birth of a daughter and had even been present when she had been born. Four years after her birth, her half-brother Alexander died. Wilhelmina would have to succeed her father, and it seemed likely that she would still be a minor. Emma would be assigned the regency in case this happened though not everyone thought that a foreign woman was the right person for the job.

Meanwhile, William's health had been deteriorating steadily. He suffered several meltdowns where he was incapable of ruling, which were most likely strokes. By early 1890, he was confined at the Loo Palace. Wilhelmina saw her father for the last time on 25 September 1890.

On 20 November 1890, Emma swore the oath as regent for her husband. During the night of the 21st, William suddenly rose from his bed, and when ordered back to his bed, he said, "Who commands here? You or I?"

Those were his last words. Over the next two days, William was in and out of consciousness.

On 23 November 1890 at 5.45 in the morning, William died at the age of 73 - leaving his ten-year-old daughter Wilhelmina as Queen.

Wilhelmina later wrote in her memoirs, "Although during the last few months his suffering was such that I could no longer visit him, this period left a deep mark on my life. The atmosphere at Het Loo was dominated by his illness. Everything became strained. When his illness was at its worst Mother spent all her time at his bedside and I hardly saw her. How much it means to a child when her mother disappears out of her life, and for such a long time! The last night she did not come to bed at all - I had been sleeping in her room for some time - and that night I felt like something terrible was happening upstairs in Father's room. People tried to hide it from me, but yet I knew what that terrible thing was. When all was over Mother came to my bed and, deeply moved, told me that Father had died."[16]

---

[16] Lonely but not alone p.23

MARCH

20 March 1934 - The death of Queen Emma

Queen (regent) Emma of the Netherlands RP-F-00-7384 via Rijksmuseum (public domain)

Queen Emma, born Emma of Waldeck and Pyrmont, was born on 2 August 1858 and was just 20 years old when she married the 61-year-old King William III of the Netherlands.

Their only daughter and the future Queen of the Netherlands was born on 31 August 1880.

When William died on 23 November 1890, Emma became regent for their 10-year-old daughter. She oversaw the education of her daughter while running the country, as a foreigner and a woman at that. She handed over the reins of government upon her daughter's 18th birthday, and by then, she looked much older than her 40 years. To thank her for her regency, the public gave her 300,000 guilders, most of which she spent on founding a tuberculosis charity - a disease which had killed her elder sister. When her daughter married in 1901, Emma moved to the Lange Voorhout Palace. She would also often spend her summers at Noordeinde Palace.

From 1909 until 1927, she was once more appointed as regent in case Wilhelmina died during the minority of her daughter Juliana. Wilhelmina's husband, Henry, was believed to be less suited to the task.

In March 1934, Emma fell ill with a cold that developed into pneumonia. When it was believed that the danger had passed, Emma quietly passed away in her sleep during the early morning of 20 March. She was 75 years old.

Wilhelmina later wrote in her memoirs, "This time, however, we soon received a telephone call from the doctor, who advised me to return immediately because Mother had suddenly fallen ill and her condition gave rise to anxiety. We left at once. A few tense days followed. Juliana and I were with her at the Voorhout day and night, and Henry paid several short visits, with the doctor's consent. On the 20th of March, God called her to Him. On the 27th, we accompanied her to her last resting-place in the vault of the Nieuwe Kerk in Delft, where she lies beside my father. Since the end of her Regency, she had devoted herself entirely to suffering humanity. The warmth of her interest and her intuitive understanding of the circumstances of those who suffered as well as of those who nursed them caused many a heart to rejoice in the course of the years. Mother's feelings went out to all, and she was a regular visitor in all classes of society."

She added, "The news of her death caused general grief and regret among our people. We were particularly moved by the small tokens of love which were laid besides her bier, and perhaps even more by the expressions of those who came to say a last farewell. We, as members of the family, were affectionately included in this spontaneous demonstration of love. At her funeral, the national anthem of Waldeck-Pyrmont was played for the last time."[17]

On 30 March, Wilhelmina wrote to her former governess Miss Winter, "For me, the sun for ever has gone, you will understand."[18] Emma was interred in the royal crypt in Delft.

---

[17] Lonely but not alone p.139-140

[18] Darling Queen - Dear Old Bones edited by Emerentia van Heuven-van Nes p.307

23 March 1897 - The death of Auntie Sophie

Princess Sophie of the Netherlands
RP-F-00-7330 via Rijksmuseum (public domain)

With her, the last of father's family had died & I am now the only direct representative of my family - would that I were a worthier one![19]

---

[19] Darling Queen, Dear old bones edited by Emerentia van Heuven-van Nes p.167

Princess Sophie of the Netherlands was born on 8 April 1824 as the daughter of the future King William II of the Netherlands and of his wife Grand Duchess Anna Pavlovna of Russia at Kneuterdijk in The Hague.

In 1840, Sophie's father finally became King of the Netherlands after the abdication of her grandfather, who went on to contract a morganatic marriage. Sophie was present during her father's inauguration. She was now 16 years old, and marriage was on the cards. On 25 January 1842, the engagement was officially approved, and she married Charles Alexander, the future Grand Duke of Saxe-Weimar-Eisenach on 8 October 1842. She was now the Hereditary Grand Duchess of Saxe-Weimar-Eisenach.

She did not become pregnant right away, leading to questions, even from her own mother. They need not have worried, and Sophie gave birth to her first child, a son named Charles Augustus, on 31 July 1844. Her parents visited Weimar, and her mother stayed by Sophie's side for six weeks. In 1849, Sophie gave birth to Marie. Anna Sophie was born in 1851 but died at the age of 8. Her last child was Elisabeth, born in 1854.

Sophie never stopped following the Dutch news and she also visited the Netherlands often. She rushed to the Netherlands to be by her father's side after his stroke. Early in 1849, Sophie's father suffered a heart attack, and she went to him as quickly as she could. As the train arrived, the bells of the church were already ringing; she had come too late. Sophie tried to support her devastated mother. Sophie's brother was now King William III of the Netherlands, albeit with the greatest reluctance. She stayed to witness her brother's inauguration and to play mediator between her mother and her sister-in-law. It was a tough time for the entire family.

Life changed when Sophie's father-in-law died in 1853, and her husband succeeded as Grand Duke. They moved into the Grand Ducal residence, while her mother-in-law moved into her widow's seat. She did everything she could to support her husband in the early years of his reign. The death of the 8-year-old Anna Sophie hit both of them hard. In early 1865, Sophie also lost her mother. She was by her mother's side when she died. Her sister-in-law, another Sophie, was also there and their relationship had never been good. Queen Sophie wrote about her dying mother-in-law, "Selfish to the last, no matter how terribly she suffers."[20]

In 1873, the first of her children was to marry. Her son Charles Augustus married his second cousin, Princess Pauline of Saxe-Weimar-Eisenach. She was their second choice, after a match with a Russian Grand Duchess fell through. Her eldest daughter Marie married Prince Heinrich VII Reuss in 1876, who was just one year younger than Sophie herself. However, Marie was in love. Sophie and her husband were desperate.

Charles Alexander wrote, "My worries turn into sadness, sadness turns into regret, and I am killing myself with worry."[21]

---

[20] Sophie in Weimar by Thera Coppens p.407

[21] Sophie in Weimar by Thera Coppens p.409

Prince Heinrich VII Reuss was clearly not good enough for their Princess. Eventually, they caved, and the engagement was announced on 8 October 1875.

Princess Pauline was soon pregnant with her first child. Sophie was going to become a grandmother. On 10 June 1876, a son named William Ernest was born. In the Netherlands, Queen Sophie was nearing death. She died on 3 June 1877 and Sophie and Charles Alexander travelled to the Netherlands to pay their respects. Queen Sophie was at last released from her unhappy marriage. She left two surviving sons behind.

Sophie's own family was growing. Pauline gave birth to a second son in 1878. Marie's first son had been stillborn, but a healthy son was born in 1878. Four more children would follow for Marie, of which three survived to adulthood. Sophie's youngest daughter Elisabeth would not marry until 1886 after refusing the chance to become Queen of the Netherlands as the wife of her uncle King William III. She was repulsed by him. William's sons would all predecease him, and he was looking for a new wife. Sophie was in favour of the idea and tried to convince her daughter. William seemed to realise her reluctance and travelled on to the Prince of Waldeck and Pyrmont, whose daughter Emma he would eventually marry.

Just after William married Emma, Prince Henry, Sophie and William's brother died. He had left no children, and the Dutch Royal House was heading to the brink of extinction. William's eldest son was still alive but unmarried as he was not allowed to marry the woman he loved. He died in 1879 in Paris. This left just one of

William's sons, Alexander. He was not considered to be mentally able to take over as King and he lived alone with a parrot. Perhaps Sophie would one day be called to ascend the Dutch throne.

After her death, she could be succeeded by her son, but the Dutch Constitution forbade that the King of the Netherlands was also the Head of State of another country. He would then have to choose between the Grand Duchy and the Kingdom. In early 1880, it was announced that Queen Emma was pregnant. On 31 August 1880, the future Queen Wilhelmina was born. The disappointment of her gender was quickly forgotten by the Dutch people, who considered anything to better than to be ruled by a German prince. In 1884, Alexander died, leaving the young Wilhelmina as the heiress.

Sophie was very fond of her young niece, and they often visited each other. Wilhelmina would later praise her for her wise counsel. Wilhelmina wrote in her memoirs, "Aunt Sophie came to stay with us every year and always loved being back in her old country. She was my last link with Father, which created a special bond between us, and she would be my successor if something should happen to me. Even at that age, I attached great importance to the fact that she was the person to whom I would leave our country. A warm friendship and mutual appreciated existed between Aunt Sophie and Mother. My aunt, who was so well informed about life in this country, was the ideal companion for Mother, who could discuss everything with her. My aunt was exceptionally gifted and had a penetrating mind. She and I were also great friends, and I have a vivid recollection of our talks in her room, which were very helpful to me. She was very intelligent, and Weimar owed her a great deal. Princess in the noblest sense of the word!"[22]

Sophie's last visit to the Netherlands was in the summer of 1896, and she stayed at Soestdijk Palace. She would die on 23 March 1897 at the age of 72. Wilhelmina wrote in her memoirs, "Towards the end of that busy winter, on the 23rd of March, we received the news of Aunt Sophie's sudden death. She collapsed in the middle of her work and died within a few hours. We felt her loss deeply after all the love we had always had from her and the advice and help she had always been prepared to give us; and she had been our last link with father. As I said before, she would have been my successor if something happened to me. Her going gave me a taste of real life; it matured me, and strengthened my sense of responsibility towards my future task."[23]

To her governess Miss Saxton Winter, she wrote, "I just want to come & tell you myself about the great grief we, mother & I, have just had: my dear Auntie Sophie had died."[24]

Wilhelmina had hoped to attend the funeral, but there was "no service where ladies could go. This is a great grief to me for I can't say how I would have liked to be present."[25]

[22] Lonely but not alone p. 44

[23] Lonely but not alone p. 54-55

[24] Darling Queen, Dear old bones edited by Emerentia van Heuven-van Nes p.165

[25] Darling Queen, Dear old bones edited by Emerentia van Heuven-van Nes p.167

APRIL

18 April 1902 - Typhoid fever comes knocking

Queen Wilhelmina and Prince Henry had been married for just a few months when she found herself pregnant for the first time. Tragically, it would be the start of many disappointments. On 9 November 1901, she suffered a miscarriage, and the cause was not clear.

Queen Wilhelmina was ordered to bed rest for four weeks and was assured that she would completely recover. She fell pregnant again early the following year, much to her delight. She wrote to her former governess Miss Winter in late March, "We will have to go without our most enjoyable visit to Amsterdam this year as I am expecting a great event if everything goes as I have reason to hope! I am beginning the 4th month just now; I write this to show you that positive certainty is not yet possible to give, but that I have all reason to hope."[26]

Wilhelmina travelled to The Loo Palace to wait out the next few months, and she arrived there on 3 April 1902. However, she soon became dizzy and took to her bed. Just one week later, doctors suspected that she was suffering from typhoid fever. Her mother Queen Emma travelled from The Hague to Apeldoorn to nurse her daughter through the illness. The diagnosis was confirmed on 18 April when the palace gates were plastered with pamphlets announcing the presence of a contagious disease.

---

[26] Darling Queen, Dear old Bones edited by Emerentia van Heuven-van Nes p.283

For two weeks, the Netherlands held their breath as the young Queen fought for her life. The fear of a German Prince inheriting the throne suddenly seemed all too close. For several days, fever ravished the Queen's body, and it wasn't until 29 April that the newspapers reported that her condition was improving. To everyone's great joy, she had survived, but her pregnancy had not remained unaffected. In early May, Wilhelmina gave birth to a stillborn son. Wilhelmina bravely told the doctor, "It is terribly sad, but I shall bear it."[27] Wilhelmina would remain afraid of infectious diseases.

In July when she was recovering in Schaumburg, she wrote to Miss Winter, "I knew all the time I was ill that my mother and others kept sending you news and I knew that your thoughts were with me."[28]

---

[27] Wilhelmina, de jonge Koningin by Cees Fasseur p. 265

[28] Darling Queen, Dear old Bones edited by Emerentia van Heuven-van Nes p.283

19 April 1876 - The life of Henry of Mecklenburg-Schwerin, Prince Consort

Prince Henry RP-F-F21072 via Rijksmuseum (public domain)

Duke Henry of Mecklenburg-Schwerin was born on 19 April 1876 as the youngest son of Frederick Francis II, Grand Duke of Mecklenburg-Schwerin, and his third wife, Princess Marie of Schwarzburg-Rudolstadt.

When he was seven years old, his father died and he was succeeded by Henry's much older half-brother who became Frederick Francis III, Grand Duke of Mecklenburg-Schwerin. The family often spent the winter months at Schwerin and the summer months at Heiligendamm or Rabensteinfelt. The latter was also intended as a dower residence for Henry's widowed mother. Henry learned to hunt at Rabensteinfelt, and it would remain one of his favourite hobbies throughout his life.

From the age of 13, Henry attended the Vitzthum gymnasium in Dresden where he turned out to be an average student. He graduated from there in 1894 and went on an extended trip to India, Sri Lanka and Greece with a schoolfriend of his, Major Alt-Stutterheim. Upon his return, he went to the military academy and was stationed in Potsdam. He had his own villa there, and he filled it with his hunting trophies. He led quite the frivolous life in Potsdam, to such an extent that when his possible match with Queen Wilhelmina came to the attention, the Dutch court investigated his past. After three years, he had risen to the rank of captain, but he did not find fulfilment in the army and requested to leave. In 1899, he went to work for the Ministry of Finance in Schwerin.

Soon, there would be another direction in his life. His mother Marie was lifelong friends with Queen Emma of the Netherlands, regent for her daughter Queen Wilhelmina until 1898 and they believed that Henry would be perfect for Wilhelmina. In early May 1900, Emma and Wilhelmina travelled to Schwarzburg for a brief holiday where the two were formally introduced. As an "alternative" Prince Frederick William of Prussia was also invited, just in case Wilhelmina didn't like Henry. Henry's brother Adolf was also invited, but he did not show up. Henry and Wilhelmina had met for the first time when Wilhelmina was just 12 years old. But no matter how much Queen Emma wanted the match with Henry, Wilhelmina had already resolutely declared that she would marry "only the man that I love."[29]

The following walk and picnic at the invitation of Henry's aunt Thekla were so agreeable to Wilhelmina that she "began to wonder if a walk hand in hand through life would be recommended."[30] Upon Wilhelmina's return to the Netherlands, she inquired into Henry's life with her friends and family. Throughout the summer, Henry did not write to her until he asked to meet with her again in the autumn. That he did not write to her is perhaps not that strange. She might have wanted to know more about him; he would undoubtedly want to know more about what it would mean to become her consort. He would have to make sacrifices.

They met again in König in October where they were able to meet in relative privacy. However, the press soon caught on. On 12 October, Henry and Wilhelmina were briefly left alone after a lunch. After just ten minutes, they agreed on an engagement. Wilhelmina later wrote in her memoirs, "The die was cast. What a relief that always is on these occasions!"[31]

---

[29] Hendrik Prins der Nederlanden by J.A. de Jonge p. 44

[30] Wilhelmina de jonge Koningin by Cees Fasseur p.215

[31] Lonely but not alone p.63

Wilhelmina returned home to the Netherlands, where the engagement was announced on 16 October 1900. A delighted Wilhelmina wrote to her former governess Miss Winter, "Oh darling, you cannot even faintly imagine how frantically happy I am and how much joy, and sunshine has come upon my path."[32]

After heavy negotiations concerning his income, his status and titles, the two were married on 7 February 1901. Henry became known as Prince Hendrik in the Netherlands, and he became Prince Consort. He was also awarded the style of "Royal Highness." Henry's initial reception in the Netherlands had been somewhat lukewarm, but his popularity grew over time. One of the defining moments for this came in 1907 when the Berlin ferry - which served the Harwich/Hook of Holland route - broke in two and sank. Henry arrived the following day to help with the recovery of the bodies, but they also found a handful of survivors on the floating stern. There had been around 144 passengers on board. Once the survivors had been brought to safety, Henry helped to care for the victims and even poured them coffee or cognac. His easy-going nature also made him popular amongst the palace servants.

Though initially a happy match, Wilhelmina and Henry would grow apart over the years. She would suffer several miscarriages and a stillbirth before finally giving birth to a healthy baby girl named Juliana in 1909.

---

[32] Darling Queen, Dear old Bones edited by Emerentia van Heuven-van Nes p.271

She was his pride and joy until the day he died, and they always remained on good terms, despite the wavering relationship between Henry and Wilhelmina.

Henry focused his attentions on several causes, such as the merging of the Dutch Boy Scout organisations, and the Dutch Red Cross and he was the happiest outside of the court protocol. However, as he was completely dependent on his wife for money, he soon found himself in money trouble and was often loaning money from others. Henry's death came rather suddenly though his health had been declining for some years. He had suffered his first heart attack in 1929. On 28 June 1934, he arrived at the office of the Red Cross in Amsterdam in the early morning. Just before ten, he suffered another heart attack. He was brought to Noordeinde Palace in The Hague by ambulance as Wilhelmina was informed of his condition. Juliana was away in England at the time. He seemed to recover but suffered another heart attack on 3 July. Wilhelmina had been away to a lunch and arrived back when he had already passed away. He had requested a white funeral and no full mourning. His funeral took place on 11 July in Delft.

His inheritance was mostly debts, and he may have left several illegitimate children as Wilhelmina paid an allowance to at least three women from her own money.[33]

---

[33] Juliana en Bernhard by Cees Fasseur p.21

In her memoirs, Wilhelmina wrote, "Long before he died my husband and I had discussed the meaning of death and the eternal Life that follows it. We both had the certainty of faith that death is the beginning of Life, and therefore had promised each other that we would have white funerals. This agreement was now observed. Hendrik's white funeral, as his last gesture to the nation, made a profound impression and set many people thinking.[...]The story of my life would become much too long if I tried to express what these two lives[34] which were cut off so shortly after one another have meant to Juliana and me. After the funeral, we went to Norway to rest and to recover, and stayed there for six weeks."[35]

---

[34] Her mother had died only months before Henry

[35] Lonely but not alone p.141

27 April 1895 - The young Queen meets the old Queen

Wilhelmina and Victoria RP-P-OB-105.773 via Rijksmuseum (public domain)

In the early morning of 27 April 1895, the royal yacht De Valk
brought two Countesses van Buren from Vlissingen to
Queenborough. The Countesses were, in fact, Queen Emma and the
14-year-old Queen Wilhelmina of the Netherlands. From
Queenborough, the Queens took the train to London where they
were received by the Prince of Wales (the future King Edward VII)
and the Duchess of Albany, who was Emma's sister.

The two Queens stayed at the Brown's Hotel at Albemarle Street. That same day, they visited the National History Museum, followed by a carriage ride through Hyde Park. The following day, they attended a service at the Church of Austin Friars, known as the Dutch church. In the afternoon, they met with the Duchess of Albany again at Claremont House after taking the train from London Waterloo.

The next two days, the young Queen spent several hours at the British Museum to continue her education. Nevertheless, there was still plenty of shopping done, and she also watched the Changing of the Guard in front of St James's Palace.

On 2 May, the Queens visited Westminster Abbey and the Houses of Parliament. On 3 May, the youngest Queen of Europe met the eldest - Queen Victoria. They had lunch together before taking a drive. Queen Victoria wrote in her journal, "Shortly before two, went downstairs to receive the Queen Regent of the Netherlands and her daughter... The young Queen, who will be fifteen in August, has her hair hanging down. She is very slight and graceful, has fine features, and seems to be very intelligent and a charming child. She speaks English extremely well, and has very pretty manners."[36] For the occasion, a now-famous photo was made, but it was, in fact, two photos photoshopped together.

The following days were again spent shopping. On 7 May, they visited the Tower of London and had lunch with the Prince and

---

[36] Wilhelmina de jonge Koningin by Cees Fasseur p. 148

Princess of Wales and their three daughters at Marlborough House. The Prince of Wales had met with Wilhelmina's half-brother William, Prince of Orange in Paris before his death but it is unlikely they discussed the past. They also went to have tea with Mary of Teck, then Duchess of York.

The following day, they visited the House of Commons, where they listened to debates. That evening, Queen Emma had dinner with Queen Victoria without Wilhelmina. On 9 May - the final day - the two Queens had a last lunch with Queen Victoria. Queen Victoria presented Wilhelmina with a signed portrait of herself as a souvenir of their meeting. The Prince of Wales also visited them on that last day. Their cover as Countesses of Buren was definitely blown by now, so they received a full honour guard as they left.

On 10 May, they were back in the Netherlands. From Friedrichshof, Queen Victoria's eldest daughter wrote to her mother, "I am very glad the visit of the Queen of the Netherlands went off so well; I should much like to see them. I have the greatest respect for Queen Emma... The young Queen must be a charming and interesting girl...[37]

In her memoirs, Wilhelmina wrote of the trip, "In 1895 Mother took me to England, for ten days or perhaps a little longer. It was not just a pleasure trip; Professor Krämer accompanied us in order to guide

[37] Beloved & Darling Child edited by Agatha Ramm p.177

me round the British Museum, where I had to see the Assyrian, Egyptian and Greek antiquities. The museum aroused little interest in me, all the other things I found very exciting. What an experience: to see London in the spring, and to have so many unexpected things happening. I suppose Mother also wanted me to meet Queen Victoria's large family, for I went on several visits with her and also accompanied her on several luncheons. The visit took on momentarily an official character when we went to pay our respects to the old Queen at Windsor, but otherwise, we were free in our movements. We saw my mother's sister, Aunt Helena, at Claremont, where I played with my cousins. We had luncheon with the future King Edward VII at Marlborough House and paid a visit to his daughter-in-law, the future Queen Mary, at St James's Palace. Her first child had not yet begun to walk at that time, and the King, who died a few years ago had not been born[38]. What a long time ago!"[39] When Queen Wilhelmina met Queen Victoria again in 1898 in Nice, she was presented with the Order of Victoria and Albert.

---

[38] She means King George VI

[39] Lonely but not alone p.51

30 April 1909 – The life of Princess Juliana

Juliana and Wilhelmina RP-F-00-7373 via Rijksmuseum (public domain)

At the end of 1908, it was announced that Queen Wilhelmina was again pregnant. By then, she had suffered two miscarriages and the stillbirth of a son. There were immediately several concerns. What would happen if Wilhelmina died in childbirth? Who would act as regent for the minor child? There were only two obvious candidates: her husband Henry and her mother Emma.

Emma would undoubtedly be preferred, not only because she already had eight years experience as regent and she was quite popular. Wilhelmina also preferred her mother as regent and early the following year, Emma was officially appointed as regent if the worst should happen.

Meanwhile, Wilhelmina's pregnancy was advancing well.

Wilhelmina spent some time writing a manual as to how the child should be raised if she died. Wilhelmina passed her due date, but labour finally began on 28 April 1909, but it was a slow labour, and Wilhelmina gave birth to a daughter just before 7 A.M. on 30 April at Noordeinde Palace.

An heir to the throne, at last. It didn't even matter to the celebrating crowds that the child was "only" a girl; anything was better than a German prince. Wilhelmina decided to feed the newborn Princess herself for nine months.

On 5 June 1909, the Princess was baptised with the names: Juliana Louise Emma Marie Wilhelmina. She received the name Juliana in honour of her ancestress Juliana of Stolberg, the mother of William the Silent.

Wilhelmina later wrote in her memoirs, "She was a strong and healthy child, always a little in advance of her age in intelligence and knowledge. I must leave it to the reader to imagine our parental happiness at her arrival after we had waited for eight years.

"Of course, she changed our lives in many ways. In summer and autumn, I considered myself exempt from many duties which had no direct bearing on my official task. As soon as I had a moment free, I lived only for my child."[40]

Juliana was nicknamed "Jula" by her family, and she became the apple of her mother's (and father's) eye.

After the birth of Princess Juliana, Queen Wilhelmina would suffer two further miscarriages. Juliana would remain their only child and thus heiress to the throne. Juliana spent her childhood between three royal palaces: The Loo Palace in Apeldoorn, Noordeinde Palace and Huis ten Bosch in The Hague. A small classroom with three carefully selected students was formed at Noordeinde Palace so that she would receive her primary education with children her own age. Wilhelmina loved showing off the young Princess during meetings with her ministers at the palace. In 1911, she wrote, "Our daughter grows like cabbage (fast) and is a lively, mobile, talkative child that notices, copies and asks endless questions."[41] Wilhelmina wanted, above all, to prevent the isolated childhood that she had had.

Although Juliana would have a relatively happy family life, her parents drifted apart during the First World War. Henry was a loving father; he enjoyed playing games with her.

The war years would be a difficult time for all of them. Henry, a German prince by birth, was torn in his loyalties and as President of the Red Cross, he was away a lot. The Netherlands was neutral during the First World War, but Wilhelmina still conferred with her ministers nearly every day. At the end of the war, Henry,

---

[40] Lonely but not alone p. 77

[41] Wilhelmina de jonge Koningin by Cees Fasseur p.316

Wilhelmina and little Juliana were driven around the Malieveld in The Hague in a carriage in celebration. Around them, several monarchies had fallen, but the Netherlands still stood firm. Emperor Wilhelm II of Germany had fled to the Netherlands in early November, something Wilhelmina could not understand. Nevertheless, he would live out his days in the Netherlands. Henry and Juliana visited him and his second wife Hermine sometimes, though her mother never did.

During her youth, Juliana was raised by governesses and nurses. She loved animals and liked to play dress up like any other child. One particular dress-up party was immortalised in a painting with her father, mother and Juliana herself dressed in 17th-century dress. Juliana had to pose for nine hours, which she hated.

Juliana's education as heir the throne would continue at a relentless pace. She would need to be ready to assume the throne at the age of 18 if it was necessary. At the age of 11, her primary education in the classroom ended. After this, she received a private education with several teachers. It was a lonely time for the young Princess, who desperately wanted siblings.

She was delighted to be allowed to attend university after her 18th birthday. Two days after her 18th birthday, her mother installed her in the Council of State and from now on she attended the Speech from the Throne in the Hall of Knights. She also received an allowance of 200,000 guilders a year, her own household and her own palace at Kneuterdijk. She would hardly ever use it. Juliana loved her university years and wanted nothing more than to be treated like any other person. She wanted real friends and made them too. Nevertheless, she was driven to classes from her villa in Katwijk, and a servant would always be waiting for her after classes. She was not allowed to take her final exams but did take three orals exams to end her studies with an honorary doctorate in 1930.

It was soon time to search for a husband for Juliana. Her mother and grandmother had both been 20 years old when they married, and Juliana was soon to be 21. Juliana herself did not consider it a priority to find a husband. She would continue to miss her university days and spent the following years in a lull.

She would suffer two losses in 1934 that would hit her hard. On 20 March, her grandmother Emma died. Just four months later, her father died. Juliana was in England with her relative Princess Alice, Countess of Athlone at the time of her father's death. Juliana had the firm belief that death was simply the start of something else, and she wrote, "Mother carefully told me today that Father had died - I long to go to her. Although, after Grandmother's death, death means nothing more to me than lovely things and I know Mother feels that as well. Father was very cheery this morning, and it happened in a second, not in her presence. Isn't it lovely, so sudden. I am so glad to know that ever since Grandmother died, every life ends happily by 'death.' I am becoming a philosopher - don't mind me."[42] He received a funeral in white to symbolise the transition to a new life.

Henry's death also gave Juliana a new role - that of President of the Red Cross.

---

[42] Juliana by Jolande Withuis p.166

The search for a husband continued relentlessly. Queen Wilhelmina may have wanted a love match for her daughter, any future husband would still need to be a protestant, healthy, foreign - preferably of equal birth - royalty but he couldn't be an heir to any throne. Wilhelmina used her Almanach de Gotha to seek out possible candidates. The rise of Hitler in Germany hindered the search as any German Prince following him was undoubtedly excluded.

By 1935, Wilhelmina was becoming desperate, but hope was nearby. Prince Bernhard of Lippe-Biesterfeld presented himself to Juliana in early 1936 during a ski-trip. He didn't quite meet all the criteria but he looked good on paper. For Juliana, it was love at first sight.

On 10 July 1936, the dashing Prince Bernhard of Lippe-Biesterfeld proposed to Princess Juliana and after some consideration, she accepted him. The engagement was meant to remain a secret for three months, but the news leaked, and so it was officially announced on 8 September. Bernhard endeared himself to the public by attempting to speak Dutch at the announcement, making the resistance against a German prince a little less. Their wedding took place on 7 January 1937 - also the wedding anniversary of King William III and Queen Emma. Their honeymoon took them all over Europe and ended in Paris, where Bernhard and his "aunt" Allene completely made over the previously rather dowdy Juliana. Allene had also brought Juliana a dietician who had helped her lose some weight and Juliana had gotten a new haircut. Wilhelmina almost didn't recognise her.

Princess Juliana RP-F-00-7520 via Rijksmuseum (public domain)

After their honeymoon, Bernhard and Juliana moved into Soestdijk Palace which they renovated to their taste. Juliana's first pregnancy was announced on 15 June 1937. Juliana was still only two months pregnant when she made the announcement herself via radio. On 31 January 1938, the future Queen Beatrix was born. It had not been an easy labour, but Juliana recovered well, and the baby was healthy. Despite now having a new baby, Bernhard spent most of the time away from his family. On 5 August 1939, Juliana gave birth to a second daughter - named Irene.

In May 1940, Germany invaded the Netherlands. Juliana and her two daughters had been sleeping in a shelter by Huis ten Bosch and Wilhelmina ordered her heir to leave the country. The initial plan was for her and her daughters to go to Paris, but that was soon no longer an option. England was plan B. On 12 May, they finally managed to board a British ship. The goodbye between mother and daughter was difficult. Bernhard accompanied his wife and daughters to England but he was an officer in the army and felt that he should be staying. Bernhard immediately returned to the Netherlands when Juliana was safely in London. The Netherlands capitulated on 15 May, and he was forced to return to England. Meanwhile, Wilhelmina had been forced to leave as well. At London Liverpool station, Bernhard and King George VI awaited her. Wilhelmina believed her daughter and granddaughters would be safer in Canada. On 2 June 1940, they boarded the Sumatra. On 17 June, she spoke on the radio, "Please do not regard me as too much of a stranger now that I have set foot on these shores which my own ancestors helped to discover, to explore and to settle. [...] Whatever you do, do not give me your pity. No woman evert felt as proud as I do today of the marvelous heritage of my own people... Pity is for the weak, and our terrible fate has made us stronger than ever before. But if you want to show us in some way that we are welcome among you, let me ask you one favour. Give us that which we ourselves shall give unto you from our most grateful hearts - give us that which just now we need more than anything else. You people of Canada and the United States, please give us your strengthening love."[43]

Despite the circumstances, Juliana felt at home in Canada, and she even had a relative there in the form of Princess Alice, Countess of Athlone. She had a freedom there she had not known before. She could go out and about without being recognised and was able to go to the movies and the public pool. Although Bernhard had remained in England, he visited her from time to time. She became pregnant again in 1941 but suffered a miscarriage in September. She was again pregnant the following year, which resulted in the birth of Princess Margriet on 19 January 1943.

On 2 August 1945, Juliana and her daughters returned to the Netherlands - a country ravished by war. Juliana resumed her position as President of the Red Cross, wanting to be useful. However, there would soon be a more important task waiting for her. Wilhelmina's health had been declining, and she wanted to abdicate. Before that, Juliana would act as regent twice. From 14 October 1947 until 1 December and again from 12 May 1948 until 30 August 1948. Just before the regencies, Juliana gave birth to her fourth and final child, a daughter named Maria Christina (first known as Marijke, later as Christina). Tragically, she was born nearly blind after Juliana contracted rubella while pregnant. This would lead to the introduction of a faith healer at court, who would nearly bring down the monarchy.

---

[43] Van Loon: Popular Historian, Journalist, and FDR Confidant by Cornelis Van Minnen p.203

Queen Wilhelmina abdicated in her daughter's favour on 4 September 1948 at the Royal Palace in Amsterdam. At noon, the balcony doors of the palace swung open, and Wilhelmina presented Juliana to the public as the new Queen with visible emotion. She shouted, "Long live our Queen!" Wilhelmina reverted back to the style and title of Her Royal Highness Princess Wilhelmina.

Two days later, on 6 September, Queen Juliana was inaugurated at the Nieuwe Kerk in Amsterdam. Before taking the oath, Juliana spoke the now-famous words, "Who am I that I get to do this?"[44] Juliana had been dreading wearing the crown, and she thought it a huge sacrifice. Her first act as Queen was to present her mother with the Military Order of William, the oldest and highest honour of the Kingdom of the Netherlands, for her actions during the Second World War. On 27 December 1949, Juliana signed the papers that recognised Indonesian sovereignty over the former Dutch colony. The illness of her youngest daughter Christina and the arrival of the faith healer Greet Hofmans affected her already strained relationship with her husband. Greet first came to Soestdijk Palace in 1948, around the time Juliana became Queen after her mother's abdication. Greet immediately promised not only to heal the poorly functioning right eye of Princess Christina but also the "dead" left eye. Her confidence won over Queen Juliana who would have done anything

[44] Juliana by Jolande Withuis p.374

for her daughter. As Greet Hofmans' influence at court grew, she became close friends with Queen Juliana, and soon their circle was expanding. Prince Bernhard soon realised that he had made a grave mistake in bringing Greet to Soestdijk. He told her that she could not stay the night any more, and it earned him the ire of his wife.

Soon there were calls to have her removed entirely from the court, but Juliana was deaf to the concerns. Juliana began to hold conferences in the Old Loo Palace, where pacifism and renunciation of the established religions were the main themes. Eleanor Roosevelt - who had been dragged along as a guest to the second conference - referred to them as a bunch of "fanatics." The situation was becoming worrying, and it was feared that Greet influenced Juliana in the political sense.

It wasn't until 1956 that the whole situation exploded in the press. Prince Bernhard had seen his marriage go to the edge of the cliff and was even told to go live with his mother by Juliana. They were headed for a divorce - which was unthinkable. It was Prince Bernhard who fought back via Der Spiegel magazine with inside information. He was only leaving Soestdijk Palace "feet first." A commission was founded to investigate the matter, and they concluded that Greet needed to leave the court.

Juliana was reluctant to let her friend go, and it appeared she was unwilling to follow the conclusions made by the commission. Nevertheless, Greet visited the court for the last time at the end of

August. In her Christmas Speech of 1956, Juliana briefly touched on the situation that had affected her so much, saying, "Why do some people attack others through devious means and with untrue claims?"

Juliana never saw Greet again, and her circle of like-minded friends slowly disappeared from the court. Christina would have a relatively normal life after receiving conventional medical care and thick glasses. Prince Bernhard would go on to father at least two illegitimate daughters; Alicia Hala de Bielefeld (born 21 June 1952) and Alexia Grinda-Lejeune (born 10 July 1967). This was only officially confirmed after Bernhard's death.

Juliana's shining moment came after the North Sea flood of 1953 where she could be the kind of Queen she wanted to be - no protocol and directly involved with the public.

During the following months, Juliana spent a lot of time in the area and the shelters. On 31 January 1956, Juliana's heir Beatrix celebrated her 18th birthday. While Juliana preferred to be addressed as "Ma'am" instead of Your Majesty, Beatrix was known to be more formal.

The year 1957 was a new beginning for Queen Juliana. She continued to visit the areas affected by the North Sea Flood, and she became more involved with visiting hospitals and youth homes. She also became the royal patron of two institutes for the blind. She wanted to be known as a socially involved Queen. She remained intensely religious, and although she no longer held the conferences, she still had some obscure ideas.

In 1962, Juliana and Bernhard celebrated their 25th wedding anniversary. They spent the day itself in Lech in Austria, but Juliana was recalled home the following after a railway disaster that would cost 93 lives and remains the worst railway accident in the history of the Netherlands That same year, Juliana was hit by a great personal loss. Her mother Wilhelmina died on 28 November, and like her father Henry, Wilhelmina had requested a funeral in white. She was interred in the Nieuwe Kerk in Delft. She and Juliana had remained in close contact after the abdication, but Wilhelmina had withdrawn to a small flat intended for staff at the Loo Palace, where she died. There was a single floral arrangement on her casket with the words, "From the resistance." There was also a flag, her Military Order of William and a bible. Her funeral was the first to be broadcast on the TV.

Juliana was now also the mother of four women of marriageable age. Her second daughter Irene was the first to find a husband, but he was the Catholic Carlist pretender to the throne of Spain, Carlos Hugo, Duke of Parma, which would cause quite the crisis. After long deliberation, Irene gave up her rights to the throne to marry him and would settle abroad with him. In 1966, the heir to the throne married German diplomat Claus von Amsberg. Although he would eventually become immensely popular in the Netherlands, his reception was cold. He had been a member of the Hitlerjugend and the Wehrmacht as a 17-year-old. Their loving engagement interview won over the hearts of many, but their wedding day still saw violent protests. In 1967, Princess Margriet married Pieter van Vollenhoven while Princess Christina married Jorge Pérez y Guillermo in 1975.

Together, they would produce a total of 14 grandchildren for Juliana and Bernhard. The future King Willem-Alexander was born in 1967. Juliana - who may have dreaded becoming Queen - had grown into her role and was perhaps even enjoying it. She loved to visit the people and also began to do more state visits. A servant later recalled, "If you recognise shortcomings in yourself, you'll accept them in others as well. Juliana had an eye for human weakness. She was a warm and natural woman for whom the rules didn't count, only the soul. She lovingly accepted people who did not fit the norm of perfection and what is right and normal."[45]

On 31 January 1980, Juliana announced that she intended to abdicate on 30 April in favour of Beatrix. The day before her official abdication, Juliana looked back on her reign with the words, "Life is beautiful but hard."[46] The following day, Juliana signed her abdication and her daughter became Queen Beatrix. Like her mother before her, Juliana returned to using the style and title of Her Royal Highness Princess Juliana. They went onto the balcony where Juliana spoke the words, "Just now, I have resigned the government. I present to you Beatrix your new Queen." But it had not been such a happy occasion as before, with riots and smoke bombs making it nearly impossible for the speeches to be heard. Republicanism was on the rise.

---

[45] Juliana by Jolande Withuis p.646

[46] Juliana by Jolande Withuis p.701

The new Queen's first official visit was with the victims of the riots in the hospital the following day.

Juliana remained in the public eye for at least ten years after her abdication, and she kept up with the news. Her focus remained on social work, and she continued to visit institutes for the disabled and the like. She was present for the anniversary of the El Al disaster in Amsterdam in 1992 and in 1995, she attended the celebration for the 50th anniversary of the liberation.

Between 1987 and 1997, Juliana's memory began to fail, much to Bernhard's annoyance. He was often rude and impatient, leading to Juliana bursting out in tears.

A friend of Juliana later said, "He was insulting and disparaging and fed her feelings of inferiority.[...] If she made a mistake or forgot something, he gave you a look like: see how forgetful she is. Like he was collecting evidence against her."[47] Yet, he remained the love of her life, and she still wished to be reconciled with him.

In 1998, Juliana broke her hip during a trip to the Keukenhof, and although she physically recovered well, her mental state took a hit as well. In 1999, she announced that she would no longer be appearing in public. She was continually nursed throughout her last years. Her memory failed her even more, and she was soon unable to recognise anyone, and she was often angry and confused. Bernhard refused to see his wife.

---

[47] Juliana by Jolande Withuis p.735

In March 2004, Juliana fell ill with pneumonia and her daughters rushed to be with her. At Irene's insistence, Bernhard also came to see his wife. Christina, who was living in New York at the time, arrived too late. On 20 March 2004, Juliana passed away "peacefully."

Juliana's funeral took place on 30 March 2004. Her body was brought from Noordeinde Palace to the Nieuwe Kerk in Delft. Her daughters dressed in white while female guests were requested to wear a white accent. Her musical daughter Christina sang, "It's a gift to be simple."

Nine months after Juliana's death, her husband Bernhard also passed away.

MAY

2 May 1945 – Queen Wilhelmina returns home from exile

Queen Wilhelmina in 1945 RP-F-00-7421 via Rijksmuseum (public domain)

Queen Wilhelmina had been forced to flee after the German invasion in 1940, and she spent most of her time in exile in England with her government. By March 1945 - the war was still going on in the northern parts of the country - Wilhelmina wanted nothing more than to return home. During a 10-day-visit organised like a military operation dubbed "Nightshade", Queen Wilhelmina returned home for the first time.

On 13 March 1945, Queen Wilhelmina stepped over a border-crossing marker made of flour at Eede in the south of the Netherlands. She had been brought there by a United States army vehicle with a single piece of luggage and a man named Baud, Princess Juliana's former secretary who had been held hostage during the war. She travelled to Breda where she moved into a house called Anneville.

On 18 March, she attended a service in the Great Church of Breda. From Anneville, she visited Tilburg, Eindhoven, Den Bosch and Maastricht. On 22 March, she fled back from Venlo to England. She had spent ten days in her beloved country, but it had not been wholly liberated yet. She wrote to the British King George VI that it was, "a most moving and touching occasion which I shall never forget."[48] She could finally return home for good on 2 May 1945, three days before the peace was officially declared. She was joined by her daughter Juliana, and the two landed at Gilze-Rijen Airport. Wilhelmina returned to the Anneville house, and in the evening of 5 May 1945, she spoke on the radio again. "Men and women of the Netherlands. Our language has no words for what is now in our hearts in these hours of the liberation of the entire Netherlands. At last, we are the masters of our own homes and castles. The enemy is defeated, from east to west and from north to south. Gone is the firing squad, the prison and the torture camp."[49]

---

[48] Wilhelmina, Krijgshaftig in een vormloze jas p.484

[49] Wilhelmina, Krijgshaftig in een vormloze jas p.485

In England, Princess Alice, Countess of Athlone, wrote to Queen Mary, "What a woman and yet so clever with her Government."[50]

---

[50] Wilhelmina, Krijgshaftig in een vormloze jas p.485

4 May 1902 – A second tragedy

When Queen Wilhelmina fell ill with typhoid fever in the middle of
April 1902, she was about five months pregnant. It was her second
pregnancy, but the first had ended in a miscarriage.

For several days, fever ravished the Queen's body, and it wasn't until
29 April that the newspapers reported that her condition was
improving. To everyone's great joy, she had survived, but her
pregnancy had not remained unaffected. A gynaecologist had been
called in, despite the original doctor having realised that the situation
was hopeless. Queen Wilhelmina was in quite a bit of pain, and her
husband Prince Henry left the room because he could not bear it
anymore.

He later wrote, "Poor Wimmy suffers a lot; the entire house suffers
with her."[51] At 10.30 P.M. on 4 May 1902, Wilhelmina gave birth to
a stillborn son. The doctors assured her that it was the typhoid fever
that had caused the stillbirth and that she would still be able to have
a healthy child. Wilhelmina bravely told the doctor, "It is terribly
sad, but I shall bear it."[52] He later wrote, "At that moment I admired
our Queen as a woman with an indescribable power of mind, as a
heroine to be pitied. I had a new regard for her that will remain until
the day I die."

[51] Wilhelmina, de jonge Koningin by Cees Fasseur p. 265

[52] Wilhelmina, de jonge Koningin by Cees Fasseur p. 265

This time, her recovery was a lot slower. She was deeply saddened to have lost another pregnancy. Prince Henry wrote how it was a double tragedy since the child was a boy. Wilhelmina went on an extended trip to her uncle in Schaumburg, but it failed to cheer her. She later wrote, "I cannot tell you how much I have gone through; I had never known a great sadness, and this was very great."[53]

From Schaumburg, she wrote to her former governess Miss Winter, "I knew all the time I was ill that my mother and others kept sending you news and I knew that your thoughts were with me. My sorrow and grief is greater than words can say, I trust to God that He may help me to be brave; you see I have a very dear husband to live for and the idea of being spared for him and thus still able to go through this world with him and be useful to him, will be the greatest help to face life with courage."[54]

---

[53] Wilhelmina, de jonge Koningin by Cees Fasseur p. 265

[54] Darling Queen, Dear old Bones edited by Emerentia van Heuven-van Nes p.283

8 May 1900 – Meeting Duke Henry

Wilhelmina and Henry RP-F-F21060 via Rijksmuseum (public domain)

"Only a German Prince will do." - Emperor Wilhelm II of Germany
in 1899

Emperor Wilhelm wasn't the only who believed that only a German Prince would do for the young Queen Wilhelmina; her mother wanted it too. But while Emperor Wilhelm preferred Frederick William of Prussia, who also happened to be a quarter Dutch as the grandson of Princess Marianne of the Netherlands (daughter of King William I), Emma preferred the two youngest sons of Frederick Francis II, Grand Duke of Mecklenburg-Schwerin - Adolf Frederick and Henry. Their sister-in-law Princess Elisabeth Sybille of Saxe-Weimar-Eisenach - married to their elder brother Duke Johann Albrecht of Mecklenburg-Schwerin - was in contact with Queen Emma. In 1896, she and her husband were invited to The Loo Palace and Soestdijk Palace. The names of her husband's half-brothers must have been mentioned during this time.

Wilhelmina had met both brothers for the first time in 1892 when she was just 12 years old. The meeting had happened at her aunt Sophie's golden wedding anniversary celebrations in Weimar but was unlikely to have made a lasting impression on the young Queen. A second meeting with Henry planned for 1898 had to be cancelled because Wilhelmina had been ill. It wasn't until May 1900 that another meeting was arranged.

From 8 May until 5 June, the two Queens were going to visit Schwarzburg, staying in the Weisser Hirsch hotel. Wilhelmina could take long walks without being seen, and she could also meet potential suitors. As Schwarzburg was also the home of Henry's maternal family, and he happened to be visiting his grandmother, she met Henry first. In return, the two Queens also visited Schloss Schwarzburg and received an invitation for a walk and picnic from

Henry's unmarried aunt Thekla. Apparently, the picnic and walk were so much fun that Wilhelmina wondered, "if a walk hand in hand through life was to be recommended."[55]

It should be noted that Henry's brother Adolf never did show his face in Schwarzburg, but the Emperor's candidate Frederick William did show his face. Wilhelmina thought he had a baby-face (they were actually only a few weeks apart in age) and quickly vetoed him. This left only Henry. Wilhelmina later wrote in her memoirs, "When he had left, a few days later, we had dinner with Grandmother Schwarzburg. I missed him very much, although it was a pleasant evening."[56]

Henry was silent for a long time after the trip to Schwarzburg and did not contact Wilhelmina again until October. They were then engaged on 12 October 1900 with Wilhelmina writing to her former governess, "Oh Darling, you cannot even faintly imagine how franticly happy I am and how much joy, and sunshine has come upon my path."[57]

---

[55] Wilhelmina de jonge Koningin by Cees Fasseur p.215

[56] Lonely but not alone p.6

[57] Darling Queen, Dear old bones edited by Emerentia van Heuven-van Nes p. 271

13 May 1940 – Queen Wilhelmina escapes to England

The Netherlands had been neutral during the First World War, but the German invasion on 10 May 1940 changed everything. Juliana and her two daughters had been sleeping in a shelter by Huis ten Bosch, and Wilhelmina ordered her heir to leave the country. The initial plan was for her and her daughters to go to Paris, but that was soon no longer an option. England was plan B.

In the early morning of 10 May, Wilhelmina issued a proclamation protesting the attack on the Netherlands and the violation of the neutrality. Huis ten Bosch, with its rural setting, was considered to be too vulnerable to an attack and so Wilhelmina moved to Noordeinde Palace, which is located in the centre of The Hague. They would spend the nights in a shelter in the gardens of Noordeinde Palace. On 12 May, Juliana and her family finally managed to board a British ship. The goodbye between mother and daughter was difficult. Bernhard accompanied his wife and daughters to England, but he was also an officer in the army and felt that he should be staying. Bernhard immediately returned to the Netherlands when Juliana was safely in London.

Queen Wilhelmina had been told by her cabinet that she should be leaving the country as well. In the early hours of 13 May, Wilhelmina received a visit from General Winkelman, who told her that the situation was dire. Wilhelmina spoke on the phone with King George VI of the United Kingdom before bursting into tears in the shelter. There was no other option left - she would need to go as soon as possible. Wilhelmina boarded the HMS Hereward at Hook of Holland and initially wanted to travel to the province of Zeeland. This turned out to be impossible, and the HMS Hereward set sail for England.

Wilhelmina later wrote in her memoirs, "Of course I was fully aware of the shattering impression that my departure would make at home, but I considered myself obliged, for the sake of the country, to accept the risk of appearing to have resorted to ignominious flight. If the guerilla against the parachute troops had not cut off all connections with the army fighting on the Grebbe, I could have joined it to share the fate of the soldier and, as William III put it, to be the last man to fall in the last ditch. I knew that this was not granted to me either."[58]

Later that day, Queen Wilhelmina arrived at Harwich, where the British authorities had already arranged for a train to London. Wilhelmina wrote, "At the station, I was met by King George and by my children, who were very upset and did not understand that I should have had to follow them so soon. The King asked me to be the guest of himself and the Queen, and escorted me to Buckingham Palace."[59]

The following day, she issued another proclamation telling the people that the government had to be moved abroad.

---

[58] Lonely but not alone p.154

[59] Lonely but not alone p.154

"Do not despair. Do everything that is possible for you to do in the country's
best interest. We shall do our best. Long live the fatherland!"[60]
On 24 May, Wilhelmina spoke on the radio for the first time. From July, the BBC broadcasted Radio Oranje (Orange) where Wilhelmina spoke 34 times over the course of the war to encourage the Dutch people. It was illegal for the Dutch people to listen to the broadcasts and many did so in secret. King George VI was most impressed by Wilhelmina, calling her "a remarkable woman and wonderfully courageous."[61] However, Wilhelmina knew she would not be able to stay in Buckingham Palace indefinitely and by the end of the month, she was looking at other possibilities. It was decided that Juliana and her children should go to Canada for their safety but Wilhelmina wanted to stay in London. Her daughter's absence hit her hand during those first few weeks and she was often, understandably, emotional.

Queen Wilhelmina eventually moved to Eaton Square 82, "a grand and dark London house."[62] While she spent most of her time in exile in England, she also visited the United States in 1942 and addressed a joint session of the United States Congress.

---

[60] Wilhelmina, Krijgshaftig in een vormloze jas by Cees Fasseur p.280

[61] Wilhelmina, Krijgshaftig in een vormloze jas by Cees Fasseur p.281

[62] Wilhelmina, Krijgshaftig in een vormloze jas by Cees Fasseur p.287

She also visited her daughter in Canada a few times, like for the baptism of Princess Margriet on 29 June 1943.

She was finally able to return to a semi-liberated Netherlands in March 1945 before returning officially on 2 May 1945.

24 May 1940 – Queen Wilhelmina speaks on the radio

On 13 May 1940, Queen Wilhelmina escaped from the invading German troops and travelled on the HMS Hereward to England. Later that day, Queen Wilhelmina arrived at Harwich, where the British authorities had already arranged for a train to London. Wilhelmina wrote, "At the station, I was met by King George and by my children, who were very upset and did not understand that I should have had to follow them so soon. The King asked me to be the guest of himself and the Queen, and escorted me to Buckingham Palace."[63]

The following day, she issued another proclamation telling the people that the government had to be moved abroad. "Do not despair. Do everything that is possible for you to do in the country's best interest. We shall do our best. Long live the fatherland!"[64]

On 24 May, Wilhelmina spoke on the radio for the first time during the war. She spoke to the Dutch overseas citizens, saying "Firstly, a word of thanks for your sympathies with the unmentionable suffering that has befallen our motherland so undeservedly and which reached its pinnacle with the occupation of our land in Europe despite the fierce resistance by our military forces supported by the cold-bloodedness of our people.

---

[63] Lonely but not alone p.154

[64] Wilhelmina, Krijgshaftig in een vormloze jas by Cees Fasseur p.280

"Their remarkable courage and determination in the most difficult of circumstances have earned them the admiration of friend and foe. Despite the experienced setback, my trust in the future remains unaltered. Our people have known troubled times before which they have overcome with their trust in God and their wish to be free. This is why I am giving you these words of encouragement. Nor my people, nor my ministers, nor I have in these dark days doubted what our duty commands. And we shall be calm and courageous, trusting in the justice in our cause. We shall all rise above the events of the moment because we follow the mainline of a great principle, the only ones who are powerful and confident and who bring along that they fight against injustice.

"Then now a word of confidence for you all overseas. For centuries we have been together, and from that, we have bonds of appreciation and affection, so strong that they, in these heavy days, are helping to support us. Our constitution has made the overseas lands to an unbreakable unit, and it is my satisfaction to say that these are not empty words. You have given this a meaning, so deep and rich, that alone is a guarantee for a better future, resting on the unity of the realm, which has remained so strong and alive. The call for help on the Dutch East Indies from the motherland has been answered by all layers of the society of the Dutch East Indies, and great sums of money have been made available to me. I thank them, from the name of the motherland, that we will never forget how the people of the Dutch East Indies have to the aide of their overseas brothers.

"Our tricolour, a symbol of peace, order, safety and enforcing the law, even for the least and the weakest, will wave proudly over the largest part of the realm. With God's help, this will remain this way until the end of days. Gather around the Governor, support him with his heavy task, move aside your difference and be of one mind because you should remember that it is about the preservation and the salvation of the Kingdom. My thoughts are with you."

The following day, she also addressed listeners in the United States and the United Kingdom. From July, the BBC broadcasted Radio Oranje (Orange) where Wilhelmina spoke 48 times over the course of the war to encourage the Dutch people. It was illegal for the Dutch people to listen to the broadcasts and many did so in secret. King George VI was most impressed by Wilhelmina, calling her "a remarkable woman and wonderfully courageous."[65] Winston Churchill described her as the only real man in all the governments in exile in London.[66]

[65] Wilhelmina, Krijgshaftig in een vormloze jas by Cees Fasseur p.281

[66] Daughter of Empire: My Life as a Mountbatten by Pamela Hicks p.146

28 May 1891 – Queen Wilhelmina's first official duty

How does one introduce a child to royal life, especially one who is already a Queen in her own right?

Queen Wilhelmina was just ten years old when she performed her first official duty. On 28 May 1891, Wilhelmina laid the foundation stone of a new hospital in Amsterdam, called the Wilhelmina Gasthuis. The weather was apparently awful, and the organisation was chaotic. When the hospital later celebrated its 75th anniversary, a bronze statue of the 10-year-old Wilhelmina, made by Mari Andriessen, was placed at the entrance. When it stopped being a hospital in 1983, the statue was moved to Academic Medical Center in Amsterdam. The old Wilhelmina Gasthuis currently consists of offices and apartments.

Shortly after the visit to Amsterdam, Queen Wilhelmina and her mother received an official visit from Emperor Wilhelm II of Germany and his wife Augusta Victoria of Schleswig-Holstein. Wilhelmina later wrote in her memoirs, "On this occasion, I had to act as hostess to the Empress, at home as well as in public. She was very kind and motherly. We followed Mother and the Kaiser in a red carriage. I also had to attend the official banquet. The days of the visit were rich in new experiences for me."[67]

Over the next two years, the young Queen laid two more foundation stones in Rotterdam and Utrecht.

---

[67] Lonely but not alone p.42-43

In June 1892, Wilhelmina also visited the capitals of the northern provinces of Friesland and Groningen. In Friesland, Wilhelmina was shown the meagre meals that a labourer survived on. During visits to Brabant and Twente, she visited textile factories and learned of the circumstances the labourers had to work in.

Wilhelmina later wrote in her memoirs, "Soon we began to pay official visits to towns and provinces, always arranged so as not to interfere with my lessons. At first, these duties frightened me, not at the moment itself but before. I became highly wrought-up about them, with the result that in spite of my perfect health I looked pale and tired during these visits, and gave the public the impression of being a weak child, which made Mother unhappy. I soon got used to the public appearances themselves; Mother made things easy for me."[68]

---

[68] Lonely but not alone p.42

JUNE

2 June 1940 – Princess Juliana departs for Canada

Wilhelmina with Juliana's family in Canada RP-F-F01307 via Rijksmuseum
(public domain)

The Netherlands had been neutral during the First World War, but the German invasion on 10 May 1940 changed everything. Juliana and her two daughters had been sleeping in a shelter by Huis ten Bosch, and Wilhelmina ordered her heir to leave the country. The initial plan was for her and her daughters to go to Paris, but that was soon no longer an option. England was plan B.

In the early morning of 10 May, Queen Wilhelmina issued a proclamation protesting the attack on the Netherlands and the violation of the neutrality. Huis ten Bosch, with its rural setting, was considered to be too vulnerable to an attack and so Wilhelmina moved to Noordeinde Palace, which is located in the centre of The Hague. They would spend the nights in a shelter in the gardens of Noordeinde Palace. On 12 May, Juliana and her family finally managed to board a British ship. The goodbye between mother and daughter was difficult. Bernhard accompanied his wife and daughters to England, but he was also an officer in the army and felt that he should be staying. Bernhard immediately returned to the Netherlands when Juliana was safely in London.

Queen Wilhelmina had been told by her cabinet that she should be leaving the country as well. In the early hours of 13 May, Wilhelmina received a visit from General Winkelman, who told her that the situation was dire. Wilhelmina spoke on the phone with King George VI of the United Kingdom before bursting into tears in the shelter. There was no other option left - she would need to go as soon as possible. Wilhelmina boarded the HMS Hereward at Hook of Holland and initially wanted to travel to the province of Zeeland. This turned out to be impossible, and the HMS Hereward set sail for England.

While Queen Wilhelmina set up a government in exile in London, it was decided that Juliana and her daughters should go to Canada for their safety. Princess Alice, Countess of Athlone, Wilhelmina's first cousin and her husband, who was the Governor-General of Canada, had offered to help. After all, England could be invaded as well. On 2 June 1940, Juliana, her daughters and several others boarded the

HNLMS SUMATRA, which was accompanied by the *HNLMS JACOB VAN HEEMSKERCK*. Juliana's husband Bernhard waved her off from Milford Haven while Queen Wilhelmina bade her daughter farewell from Lydney Park. Wilhelmina later wrote in her memoirs, "I gazed after the car as it drove off from Lydney Park - when and where would we meet again? Bernhard returned late in the evening, very unhappy at the prospect of their long separation. Several weeks passed before Juliana's first letter brought a ray of light for him and myself."[69] They arrived safely on 10 June 1940 and stayed at Government House at first. A month and a half later, they moved to a villa in Ottawa.

Juliana often wrote to her mother and her husband in England. It would be a long time before she would see them again. Wilhelmina wrote to her daughter, "Your letters are my lungs that will allow me to breathe to continue to live and work."[70] Juliana was kept informed of state business, she would need to be able to take over if it ever came to it after all. Their letters went by diplomatic post.

They would not meet again until June 1942. Wilhelmina wrote, "Our happiness at seeing each other again was indescribable. How I enjoyed Juliana's charming house in Rockliffe Park, in the middle of the woods overlooking a little lake."[71]

---

[69] Lonely but not alone p. 156

[70] Wilhelmina, Krijgshaftig in een vormeloze jas by Cees Fasseur p.284

[71] Lonely but not alone p. 181

Bernhard also visited Canada several times. At the end of 1942, Juliana moved to Stornoway, which was a little bigger. By then, she was expecting her third child - Princess Margriet. Juliana also visited the United States several times and met with President Roosevelt, who was quite proud of his Dutch roots. During his inauguration in 1933, he swore the presidential oath on his Dutch family bible. Juliana was concerned with the life her husband led in England and he hardly ever wrote to her about it. It will come as no surprise that he had an affair, and even though he never mentioned her by name, it is likely to be Ann, Lady Orr-Lewis, the wife of Sir Duncan Orr-Lewis. Bernhard later confirmed in an interview that Juliana knew about it and after the war, Ann sometimes went skiing with the entire family. After the war, he would father two daughters with two different women, and he later acknowledged them.

Juliana left Canada for England in September 1944, but there was little she could do there. In March 1945, Queen Wilhelmina made her first visit to the partially-liberated Netherlands. Juliana would have to wait a little bit longer. In June 1945, she travelled to the United States with 15,000 American troops, and she was deeply touched by their reception in New York.

On 2 August 1945, Juliana and her three daughters landed at Teuge Airport near Arnhem. The years of exile were over.

3 June 1877 - The death of Sophie of Württemberg

Sophie of Württemberg, Queen of the Netherlands RP-P-OB-4899 via Rijksmuseum (public domain)

Although Queen Wilhelmina of the Netherlands obviously never knew her father's first wife, Sophie's death opened up the possibility of his remarriage and the eventual birth of Wilhelmina.

Sophie of Württemberg was born in Stuttgart on 17 June 1818 as the daughter of King William I of Württemberg and his second wife Catherine Pavlovna of Russia. She married her first cousin William, future Prince of Orange and future King William III of the Netherlands in Stuttgart on 18 June 1839. She considered herself to be more intelligent than him and thought she could dominate him. She became Princess of Orange upon the abdication of King William I of the Netherlands in 1840. Sophie and her husband William never got along. The births of their sons changed nothing. They had three sons, William in 1840, Maurice in 1843 and Alexander in 1851. Sophie became Queen consort in 1849 when King William II died suddenly. By then, William and Sophie were on the brink of a separation. Their second son Maurice suffered from meningitis, and they quarrelled by his sickbed. Sophie wanted to consult another doctor, but William refused. Maurice ultimately died of the illness. In 1855, they separated for good, but divorcing was not an option. William was given custody of their eldest son and Sophie was allowed to keep their youngest son Alexander until he was nine years old. Sophie would also have to continue to fulfil her duties as Queen.

From 1855, she lived mostly in Huis ten Bosch, and she went to visit her father almost every year. She was also a regular visitor to Emperor Napoleon III and his wife, Eugénie. She corresponded with intellectuals, who praised her. Historian John Lothrop Motley wrote, "The best compliment I can pay her is, that one quite forgets that she is a queen, and only feels the presence of an intelligent and very attractive woman."

Sophie's health deteriorated in early 1876. On 7 January 1876, she had arrived in Paris while already ill, and she had to be carried to her apartments. She continued her travels towards to Cannes, where she hoped to feel better. Her doctors reported that she suffered from 'fièvre paludiène' (malaria), tiredness, tightness in her chest, and coughing attacks. These reports were published in the newspapers. William thought the entire reporting on her health was ridiculous and believed she only wanted the attention. When she felt a little better, she wrote, "The King cannot forgive me that I didn't die, as he had expected. He never comes to me, never asks how I am. When I was so very ill last time, he sang and had someone loudly play the piano under my bedroom."[72]

Sophie would not recover from her next illness. During the spring of 1877, it became clear that the end was near. On 2 June 1877, one newspaper reported, "From The Hague, we received, this morning at 11, the sad message that Her Majesty The Queen is dying."[73] This time, her husband did bother to go to her at Huis ten Bosch.

Sophie died on 3 June 1877 just before noon, and the following autopsy showed that her bowels, gallbladder, liver and lungs had all been infected. It had been a miracle that she lived as long as she did. Newspapers reported, "The entire Netherlands mourns the death of their beloved Queen." On her deathbed, she wore her wedding veil, believing that she had died the day of her wedding.

Sophie, Queen of the Netherlands, was buried on 20 June in the Nieuwe Kerk in Delft. King William, their two sons and Prince Henry and Prince Frederick were all there.

---

[72] Willem III by Dik van der Meulen p.529

[73] Willem III by Dik van der Meulen p.529

William stayed in the church while the others went down into the crypt. The palace of Huis ten Bosch was immediately closed after Sophie's death and it stood empty for a long time. Her husband remained in The Hague until 29 June when he left for Paris with a certain Mademoiselle Ambre.

7 June 1917 - Train accident at Houten

On 7 June 1917, Queen Wilhelmina was travelling from Den Bosch to The Hague, and her two royal coaches were attached to the back of a regular train service. She was in her saloon car when eleven of the coaches derailed, and one even rolled off the embankment. The train had broken up in parts, with the front part remaining standing. Fortunately, the royal coaches remained standing as well, though they did come off the rails. Queen Wilhelmina remained unharmed, but the damage was enormous. Queen Wilhelmina helped to care for the 26 wounded with the aid of a British man. No one was killed in the accident, which seems like a miracle if you look at the photos. The only related death appears to have been the stillbirth of a baby later that day of a heavily pregnant woman who had been on the train. The cause of the derailment was probably the expansion of the tracks due to the heat.

A railway worker reported, "I soon saw the entire train off the rails. Because we came from behind, we reached the royal carriages first. Just then, the Queen alighted. Exactly, sir, like nothing had happened. To a lady of her entourage, she yelled, "Fetch my first-aid kit and the bottle of Eau de Cologne next to it". With a crowbar, I opened the door of the following carriages. My buddy and I were the first to get a splash of Eau de Cologne on our dirty handkerchiefs and then the Queen went to work." Queen Wilhelmina used the Eau de Cologne on a woman who had lost consciousness.[74]

---

[74] https://historiek.net/treinongeluk-houten-1917-koningin-wilhelmina/68560/

Queen Wilhelmina boarded the front part of the train with several other passengers, and they were brought to Utrecht. The Queen was praised for her calm appearance and bravery.

Congratulations on her survival soon began pouring in, and various royal palaces had registers where people could congratulate her.

11 June 1879 - The death of William, Prince of Orange

William, Prince of Orange RP-F-F00815-35-4 via Rijksmuseum (public domain)

Queen Wilhelmina of the Netherlands would never know her elder half-brother as he died a year before she was born, but for a long time, it was he who was meant to be King.

William was born on 4 September 1840, shortly before the abdication of his great-grandfather, King William I of the Netherlands. He was thus born third in the line of succession, behind his grandfather and father. Being yet another William, he was nicknamed Wiwill in the family. His parents were the future King William III of the Netherlands and his first wife, Sophie of Württemberg. His parents were famously mismatched, and he would grow up in an evergrowing battle. Yet, they managed to have two more sons. Maurice was born in 1843, but he would die in childhood. Alexander was born in 1851.

William grew up to be quite the hothead, and his mother spoiled him much to his father's dismay. Perhaps it is no surprise as he was often witnessing violent arguments. Once, Sophie had to wear long gloves for weeks after her husband scratched her arms. From the age 7, William's day was planned out to the minute for his education. In 1849, his grandfather died quite suddenly, and his father reluctantly became King William III. Young William was now formally the heir to the throne and the Prince of Orange. His more delicate younger brother Maurice fell ill with meningitis in early 1850, and he died at the age of six on 4 June 1850. His devastated mother left to take a cure, and William was left with his governor. His father found solace with a mistress.

Nevertheless, his warring parents managed to make up long enough for Sophie to fall pregnant for the third time. As the situation in the palace deteriorated, it was decided to send William to boarding school.

Despite Sophie's despair of William's leaving, the boarding school actually did him some good. Sophie's visits to him were limited, and his behaviour seemed to improve. However, he wasn't able to make many friends there. He left the school in 1854, and he then attended

Leiden University for two years. By then, his parents were officially separated, but they would never divorce.

In 1861, William was introduced to Princess Anne Murat, a granddaughter of Caroline Bonaparte and Joachim Murat, but if a marriage was the intended goal, it never took place. Likewise, Princess Alice, daughter of Queen Victoria, was considered for him. Meanwhile, William joined the army, but it did little to repair the bad reputation he had already built up, and the relationship with his father was famously bad. The city of Paris had stolen William's heart, and he would spend most his time there. Stories of his escapades there soon made the papers. He was mocked with cartoons and even received the nickname Prince Citron for his notoriously moody behaviour. His mother was soon writing to a friend that she did not expect her son ever to marry. His younger brother Alexander was known to be delicate and was also expected never to marry. Yet, King William did not want to think about the succession, according to Sophie. He was healthy enough and would probably live quite a long time. However, it was becoming a growing problem. King William's only surviving brother Henry was childless and his elderly uncle Frederick had just two daughters. King William's sister Sophie's descendants would lead to a German prince becoming King of the Netherlands, something nobody wanted.

However, young William did have a bride in mind, but she wasn't quite up to everyone's standard. Her name was Anna Mathilda - Mattie - Countess of Limburg Stirum. His father would never allow a marriage to a Dutch noblewoman, only a woman of royal blood would do. And so William partied his worries away in Paris while going into huge debts. He would return to the Netherlands just once more, for the funeral of his mother. On 7 January 1879, King William remarried to Emma of Waldeck and Pyrmont. Emma would never meet her stepson. In the late spring, the younger William became seriously ill with pneumonia. He died on 11 June 1879 in the arms of his chamberlain; he was still only 38 years old. His position as heir and the title of Prince of Orange passed to his younger brother Alexander. He would die almost five years later to the day, leaving the four-year-old Wilhelmina as the heir.

21 June 1884 - The death of Alexander, Prince of Orange

Alexander, Prince of Orange RP-P-OB-105.761 via Rijksmuseum (public domain)

Queen Wilhelmina of the Netherlands had three elder half-brothers, but she would not know any of them. The three sons of the marriage of her father, King William III of the Netherlands and his first wife Sophie of Württemberg, were William (nicknamed Wiwill), Maurice and Alexander. Maurice fell ill with meningitis in early 1850, and he died at the age of six on 4 June 1850. Though William and Sophie's marriage was famously unhappy, they managed to reconcile long enough for Sophie to fall pregnant again. Alexander was born on 25 August 1851. His elder brother William had become Prince of Orange, the title for the heir to the throne, in 1849 when their father became King.

The birth was a little premature, and Sophie took a long time to recover. She was initially feverish and restless, as was her young son. It soon became apparent that young Alexander was the opposite of his lively elder brother William. Sophie worried about him and spoiled him. As he grew older, Sophie admitted that he was "a strange boy with a character filled with contrasts."[75] He wasn't sent to school and was instead homeschooled by his overbearing mother. When travelling, the pair often visited areas known for their good air. Doctors did not give any conclusion as to what, if anything, was wrong with Alexander, but Sophie concluded that he was facing "a life of misery."[76] He had a growth spurt in 1867 that left him with a slightly curved spine.

After his 18th birthday, he also travelled to spas without his mother. At the end of 1869, he even went on a long trip onboard a naval ship to the Mediterranean. Sophie was devastated and wrote, "My boy is leaving in the first week of December, and since the date has been

---

[75] Alexander, de vergeten kroonprins by Fred J. Lammers p.22

[76] Alexander, de vergeten kroonprins by Fred J. Lammers p.27

set, it feels like my death sentence has been signed."[77] He also took classes at university but never graduated.

In 1874, Alexander moved into his own palace in The Hague, but by the end of the year, he was off travelling again. His mother hoped that he would meet a nice and suitable Princess, and she focused on Princess Thyra of Denmark. This match never took place. Sophie wrote, "My sons are well. If only they would get married, then I would have no reason to complain."[78] His elder brother William had fallen in love with a Dutch Countess and his father absolutely refused to give his permission for their marriage. William moved away to Paris, where he lived a debauched lifestyle.

On 3 June 1877, Alexander lost his mother. He was devastated and wrote, "I am now so lonely and abandoned in this big world that your affection is a support to me to keep walking the path of life. My life is broken, my happiness, my daily life, the conversations with my beloved and lamented mother - destroyed."[79] Sophie laid in state for three days and Alexander refused to leave her side. As her coffin was lowered into the crypt at Delft, Alexander threw himself onto the coffin as he wept. William, whose return to the Netherlands for the funeral of his mother would be the last visit, had to pull him off. From then on, Alexander began to save everything that had

[77] Alexander, de vergeten kroonprins by Fred J. Lammers p.31

[78] Alexander, de vergeten kroonprins by Fred J. Lammers p.55

[79] Alexander, de vergeten kroonprins by Fred J. Lammers p.61

something to do with his mother.

In his loneliness, his thoughts returned to marriage, and this time the focus was on Frederica of Hanover, but she was in love with someone else. Alexander gave up all thoughts of marriage and wrote, "Give me the freedom to walk my lonely path of life alone. I know very well that with the passing of my dear mother, I am now completely alone in the world."[80] He began collecting butterflies and miniatures, slowly turning his palace into a museum. He wrote, "My sadness has had a strange development."[81]

King William III was also thinking of marrying again, much to the dismay of his sons. Alexander saw the remarriage as an insult to his late mother, but he kept the high ground and remained polite. He was not present for the wedding of King William and Emma of Waldeck and Pyrmont in Arolsen in January 1879. He left for France and told his staff to keep the palace windows shut as a sign of mourning. When he returned, he refused to meet Emma. On 11 June 1879, his elder brother William died in France at the age of 38. Alexander was summoned and placed a picture of their mother in his brother's hands. Alexander now became the new Prince of Orange.

As the new Crown Prince, Alexander requested a meeting with his father, but he also unwillingly came face to face with his new stepmother.

---

[80] Alexander, de vergeten kroonprins by Fred J. Lammers p.63

[81] Alexander, de vergeten kroonprins by Fred J. Lammers p.63

He decided against leaving and bowed for her. However, they don't have a conversation as Alexander was rather angry with his father for putting him in this situation. To escape the situation, Alexander went to stay with his aunt Marie of Württemberg in Switzerland. He refused to appear at the opening of parliament, and a following newspaper article was personally rebuffed by Alexander. His speaking to the press led to quite a commotion, and newspapers quickly sold out. He withdrew into his own palace even more, and his parrot and dog were his only companions.

On 31 August 1880, Emma gave birth to Alexander's half-sister Wilhelmina. Alexander would never meet her. By May 1884, Alexander was seriously ill with typhoid fever. King William was in Karlsbad while Emma and Wilhelmina were spending time in Kissingen, and none of them seemed too concerned with Alexander's health. On 3 June, the first newspaper reports appeared. Despite his illness, Alexander ordered wreaths to be placed on his mother's coffin on the anniversary of her death. When William was finally informed that Alexander was probably dying, he was convinced by his doctors to stay in Karlsbad. Alexander ordered his brother William's bed – the one in which he had died - to be brought to him so that he could die in it as well.

The end came on 21 June 1884. His last words were, "Help me, please help me. I can take no more."[82]

---

[82] Alexander, de vergeten kroonprins by Fred J. Lammers p.192

He died at 2 in the afternoon. King William ordered the windows at Noordeinde Palace to be shut. However, he delayed his return to the Netherlands, and so Alexander remained unburied for nearly a month. He was finally interred in Delft on 17 July. King William was the first to leave the funeral. With his death, King William now had just one living legitimate child... Wilhelmina.

Noordeinde Palace

Photo by author

The Loo Palace

Photo by author

Entrance to the royal crypt in the Nieuwe Kerk in Delft

Photo by author

Soestdijk Palace

Photo by author

JULY

3 July 1934 – The death of Prince Henry

Emma, Juliana, Henry and Wilhelmina RP-F-00-7459 via Rijksmuseum (public domain)

Born Duke Henry of Mecklenburg-Schwerin on 19 April 1876 as the youngest son of Frederick Francis II, Grand Duke of Mecklenburg-Schwerin, and his third wife, Princess Marie of Schwarzburg-Rudolstadt, he became Prince Consort of the Netherlands as the husband of Queen Wilhelmina of the Netherlands.

Although their marriage was happy at first, over time, the couple drifted apart. Their only surviving child, the future Queen Juliana, was the apple of her father's eye.

Henry's death came rather sudden though his health had been declining for some years. He had suffered his first heart attack in 1929. On 28 June 1934, he arrived at the office of the Red Cross in

Amsterdam in the early morning. Just before ten, he suffered another heart attack. He was brought to Noordeinde Palace in The Hague by ambulance as Queen Wilhelmina was informed of his condition. Their daughter Juliana was away in England at the time. He seemed to recover but suffered another heart attack on 3 July. Wilhelmina had been away to a lunch and arrived back when he had already passed away. Wilhelmina herself informed her daughter in England and later told a courtier that her daughter had been calm. "We are brave people, who don't wail."[83] Later that day, Queen Wilhelmina made the official announcement: "It has pleased God to call my beloved husband to him. This afternoon, he passed away calmly but suddenly. I announce this with the greatest sadness. I am convinced you will share in mine and my daughter's sorrow."[84]

Juliana had the firm belief that death was simply the start of something else, and she wrote, "Mother carefully told me today that Father had died - I long to go to her. Although, after Grandmother's death, death means nothing more to me than lovely things and I know Mother feels that as well. Father was very cheery this morning, and it happened in a second, not in her presence. Isn't it lovely, so sudden. I am so glad to know that ever since Grandmother died, every life ends happily by 'death.'

---

[83] Juliana by Jolande Withuis p.166

[84] Vorstelijk begraven en gedenken. Funeraire geschiedenis van het huis Oranje-Nassau by Cees van Raak p. 78

"I am becoming a philosopher - don't mind me."[85]
Juliana took the night boat to Hook of Holland, and Wilhelmina was there to pick her up when she arrived in the morning. Juliana made sure the rings he had worn were put back on his fingers and had his favourite Huguenot cross put around his neck. She also put a bouquet of red roses in his coffin. She also requested her father's favourite clock with little horseheads from the Loo Palace and had it put into her own room.

In her memoirs, Wilhelmina wrote, "Long before he died my husband and I had discussed the meaning of death and the eternal Life that follows it. We both had the certainty of faith that death is the beginning of Life, and therefore had promised each other that we would have white funerals. This agreement was now observed. Hendrik's white funeral, as his last gesture to the nation, made a profound impression and set many people thinking.[...]The story of my life would become much too long if I tried to express what these two lives[86] which were cut off so shortly after one another have meant to Juliana and me. After the funeral, we went to Norway to rest and to recover, and stayed there for six weeks."[87]

---

[85] Juliana by Jolande Withuis p.166

[86] Her mother had died only months before Henry

[87] Lonely but not alone p.141

23 July 1906 - A third tragedy

With Wilhelmina's marriage to Henry of Mecklenburg-Schwerin on 7 February 1901, she and her mother both fervently prayed for healthy children to continue their line. Tragically, Wilhelmina would go on to suffer five miscarriages and only one healthy child was born to Wilhelmina and Henry.

In the spring of 1906, Wilhelmina was pregnant for the third time. Her first pregnancy had ended in a miscarriage at the end of 1901. Her second pregnancy ended in the stillbirth of a son following a bout of typhoid fever in 1902. Wilhelmina kept her pregnancy a secret from anyone outside of the family and only wrote to her former nanny De Kock on 19 July 1906, "My enemies, the papers, have written a lot about me, long before they had a reason for it. I can tell you now, although they are way too early, that the rumour they are spreading is true."[88]

On 4 July 1906, Wilhelmina wrote to her mother about the birth of a son to Crown Princess Cecilie of Germany (Cecilie of Mecklenburg-Schwerin) and Crown Prince Wilhelm. "Such a happiness for her, her husband, and the Emperor!" Cecilie had given birth just over a year of getting married.

Wilhelmina took to her bed following a garden party, and a "fausse couche"(miscarriage) took place on 23 July. On the 25th, newspapers reported, "A minor disposition of Her Majesty The

---

[88] Wilhelmina de jonge Koningin by Cees Fasseur p.278

Queen during some days has thwarted hopes that had been cherished for a while. The condition of Her Majesty does not give cause for concern."[89] Her private secretary reported that Wilhelmina was "very well and even cheerful."[90]

Despite her cheerfulness, the pressure must have been getting to her. She had been married for five years and had suffered three losses. The prospect of a German Prince on the throne began to loom.

---

[89] Nederlandsche Staatscourant 25 July 1906

[90] Wilhelmina de jonge Koningin by Cees Fasseur p.278

28 July 1878 - The meeting between King William and Princess Emma

Photo by author

The baroque Schloss Pyrmont was the scene of one of the most famous lines in Dutch royal history.

King William III of the Netherlands arrived here on 28 July 1878 to court Pauline of Waldeck and Pyrmont. Pauline rejected the elderly King but her sister Emma supposed exclaimed, "We cannot just let the poor man go home alone!"[91] Emma and William were 41 years apart in age and he was almost 14 years older than her own father.

---

[91] Koning Willem III by Dik van der Meulen p.565

Nevertheless, she must have seen something in him that others did not see. Even Queen Victoria wrote of him that he was "not an enviable relation to have."[92] Just three years later, she wrote of Emma and William, "The King of the Netherlands is as quiet and unobtrusive as possible; a totally altered man and all owing to her. She is charming, so amiable, kind, friendly and cheerful."[93]

One of the men accompanying the King later wrote of the four days they spent in Pyrmont, "One of the days we spent in Pyrmont, I had the honour of accompanying the Princesses (Emma and Pauline) and the King on a wonderful carriage ride, and we also went up on a marvelously high watchtower. One can say that the love had not given the King wings but it certainly gave him legs for he was normally slow and made himself comfortable and he now climbed the dozens of steps leading to the top of the tower."[94]

In any case, after the second visit in September, the engagement between Emma and William was announced and they were married early the following year. The birth of their daughter Wilhelmina completed the new family.

[92] Beloved Mama edited by Roger Fulford p.34

[93] Beloved Mama edited by Roger Fulford p.118

[94] Koning Willem III by Dik van der Meulen p.565

28 July 1940 - The first broadcast of Radio Orange

On 13 May 1940, Queen Wilhelmina escaped from the invading German troops and travelled on the HMS Hereward to England. Later that day, Queen Wilhelmina arrived at Harwich, where the British authorities had already arranged for a train to London. Wilhelmina wrote, "At the station, I was met by King George and by my children, who were very upset and did not understand that I should have had to follow them so soon. The King asked me to be the guest of himself and the Queen, and escorted me to Buckingham Palace."[95]

The following day, she issued another proclamation telling the people that the government had to be moved abroad. "Do not despair. Do everything that is possible for you to do in the country's best interest. We shall do our best. Long live the Fatherland!"[96]

On 24 May, Wilhelmina spoke on the radio for the first time during the war. From 28 July, the BBC broadcast Radio Oranje (Orange) where Wilhelmina spoke 48 times over the course of the war to encourage the Dutch people. Radio Orange was broadcast for 15 minutes and began with the words, "Radio Orange Here, the voice of a combatant Netherlands."[97]

---

[95] Lonely but not alone p.154

[96] Wilhelmina, Krijgshaftig in een vormloze jas by Cees Fasseur p.280

[97] De Oranjes in de Tweede Wereldoorlog by Carel Brendel p.80

During her first broadcast, she spoke the following words;

"I am delighted that thanks to the benevolent cooperation of the English authorities, this Dutch quarter-hour has been incorporated into the broadcasts of British radio, and I express the hope that many fellow countrymen, wherever they may be, will now be faithful listeners of the patriotic thoughts that reach them along this way. And now I am delighted to be the first to speak to you in these fifteen minutes.

"First of all, I would like to commemorate with you all the Fatherland, so deeply affected by the calamity of war. We commemorate the untold suffering that has come upon our people and that it is now constantly experiencing. We want to pay tribute to the heroes, who fell victim to their duty in the defence of our Netherlands, tribute to the courage of our resistance, which on land, at sea and in the air, with the effort of her utmost strength, have been able to withstand a much stronger assailant much longer than he expected.

"After all that has already been said and written about the war in which we are wrapped up, you will certainly not expect that I will deal briefly with the war itself and the many issues related to it. But we must realise that the war increasingly reveals its true character, as being in its deepest essence a battle between good and evil, a battle between God and our conscience on the one hand and the dark powers that reign supreme in this world. It is a struggle - which I need to tell you - belongs in the spiritual world and is fought deeply hidden in the heart of man, but which has now emerged in the most appalling way in the form of this great worldly struggle, of which we are the unfortunate victims and which causes suffering to all nations. This war is all about giving the world a guarantee that those who want good will not be prevented from accomplishing it. Those who believe that the spiritual values acquired by mankind can be destroyed by the edge of the sword must learn to realise its vanity. Crude violence cannot deprive people of their convictions.

"As in the past neither gun violence, nor the flames of the pyre, nor the impoverishment and suffering of our sense of freedom, our freedom of conscience and our freedom of faith have ever been able to wipe us out, so I am convinced that even in the present age we and all who think as we do - whatever people they may belong to - are strengthened from this trial and through all that is sacred to them and we will rise.

"That it is for this lofty purpose that thousands of our brave have already made the sacrifice of their lives and that this sacrifice has not been in vain, for the comfort of their relatives and for all of us. Although the enemy has also occupied the national soil, the Netherlands will continue the battle as long as a free happy future appears before us. Our beloved tricolour flies proudly on the seas, in the larger Netherlands in East and West; and side by side with our allies, our men continue the battle. The parts of the Overseas Empire, which so aptly expressed their compassion for the disaster that struck the Motherland, are more closely than ever associated with us in their thinking and feeling. In unbreakable unity, we want to maintain our freedom, our independence and the territory of the entire Empire. I implore my countrymen in the Fatherland and wherever they are to continue to trust, no matter how dark and difficult the times are, in the final victory of our cause, which is strong not only by the strength of arms but no less by the realisation that it concerns our most sacred goods. I have said."[98]

For the first few years, her speeches were recorded on a gramophone record which was then played by the BBC. From March 1942, she began to speak live from the studio. She wrote her own speeches and often worked for hours on them.

It was illegal for the Dutch people to listen to English radio and the Nazis eventually demanded everyone to turn in their radio. Many kept their radios to be able to listen to the broadcasts as they also often included coded messages for the resistance. After the war, Wilhelmina was criticised for not putting enough emphasis on the plight of the Jewish people.

Wilhelmina later wrote of her broadcasts, "My broadcast speeches were not only concerned with the new times. They also aimed at inspiring and stiffening resistance against the oppressor and at informing the nation of the government's policy. At the same time, I did what I could to assist my countrymen in their spiritual struggle and paid homage to those who have given their lives in the great cause."[99]

---

[98] https://nl.wikisource.org/wiki/Radiotoespraken_Wilhelmina/28_juli_1940

[99] Lonely but not alone p.172

AUGUST

1 August 1886 – The education of a Queen

Princess Wilhelmina in 1888 RP-F-F21094 via Rijksmuseum (public domain)

When the future Queen Wilhelmina was born on 31 August 1880, her elder half-brother Prince Alexander, Prince of Orange was still alive - as was her uncle Prince Frederick of the Netherlands. Under the semi-salic law in the Netherlands, she was thus third in the line of succession. However, Prince Frederick died in 1881, leaving two daughters - Louise and Marie. Prince Alexander was unmarried and sickly, and he too died in 1884. Wilhelmina was now the heiress to the throne and was set to become the first Queen regnant of the Netherlands. But how does one educate a Queen? Especially one that would be expected to rule from a young age - her father was already 63 years old when she was born.

From her early youth, Wilhelmina had been raised bilingual - in French and Dutch. On 1 August 1886, an English governess named Miss Elizabeth Saxton Winter was employed, and Wilhelmina would grow very fond of her, and they would keep in touch for the rest of Miss Winter's life. She set out to "train your character, to make a bold and noble woman out of you, unflinching and strong."[100] Most of all, Wilhelmina would be taught a sense of duty and perseverance. Wilhelmina grew up an only child but sometimes other children were invited to the Palace.

However, when it became clear that her father would not live to see her 18th birthday, her education was sped up. Her education focused on three languages, French, German and English but also included subjects just for her, like constitutional law and the organisation of the army. Her teacher was Frederik Gediking, who ran a county school in The Hague. He sometimes found it difficult to formally address his special student, and he was not allowed to shake her hand. Miss Winter attended all the lessons with Wilhelmina.

In 1890, her father died at the age of 73 and Wilhelmina became Queen at the age of 10. Her mother Emma would act as her regent until her 18th birthday.

---

[100] Wilhelmina - de jonge Koningin by Cees Fasseur p.87

From now on, Emma made sure Wilhelmina was seen as the future of the monarchy. Between 1892 and 1896, she and Wilhelmina visited every major city and providence in the Netherlands. Emma also took it upon herself to become her daughter's teacher in religious matters.

Queen Wilhelmina skating on ice in 1893 RP-F-F01233 via Rijksmuseum (public domain)

From August 1890, lessons were intensified with a more teachers Dr J.J. Salverda de Grave, F.J.L Krämer, P.J. Blok and C.M. Kan. Emma wanted her to learn history, especially Dutch history, because she believed it was the only way for Wilhelmina to know her people as she was so separated from them by protocol and etiquette. By 1896, her basic education was considered to be completed. The following two years would focus mainly on her constitutional duties. When she took up her duties, she was by far the best-educated 18-year-old in the Netherlands. However, it had been a lonely childhood surrounded by people who were much older than her. She later wrote in her memoirs, "Most of the lessons were interesting and there were breaks at the right moment, just when I began to feel tired. My secondary and academic education were combined. I never went beyond secondary level in science and foreign languages (French, German and English). My favourite subjects were Dutch and history."[101]

[101] Lonely but not alone p.49

1 August 1884 - Queen Emma's regency law

Queen regent Emma RP-P-OB-105.709 via Rijksmuseum (public domain)

After the death of Alexander, Prince of Orange, it became clear that it would be Wilhelmina who would succeed her father, and she would probably be a minor too. A regent would be required, and the Dutch Constitution demanded that a situation like that should be dealt with in a new law.

The last time this had been done was in 1850 when King William III's sons were still minors. Back then, his brother Prince Henry was designated as regent, but he had now died as well. A conclusion was soon reached, Emma should be appointed regent - she really was the only viable option. However, even King William had his doubts, though he eventually agreed. The law designating Emma as regent was approved with a large majority of 97 to 3 on 1 August 1884. Emma would rule as Queen Regent from the death of her husband until Wilhelmina's 18th birthday (at the time all other Dutch people did not reach their majority until their 23rd year).

The three people who voted against the law would have preferred to see a man act as regent, though they failed to say who that man should be. And Emma was not only a woman, but she was also a foreigner and quite young. They were not convinced that Emma knew the Netherlands well enough to be able to rule it.[102]

On 20 November 1890, as William lay dying, Emma was called for the regency in her husband's name. It was clear that he would not recover this time. He died in the early hours of 23 November with only Emma and Count Dumonceau by his bedside. The ten-year-old Wilhelmina officially succeeded him as Queen of the Netherlands but on 8 December 1890, Emma swore an oath in front of the States-General as regent and as her custodian.

The text of the oath as per the current law of 1994 goes as follows, "I swear allegiance to the King[103], I swear that I will maintain and

---

[102] Wilhelmina, de Jonge Koningin by Cees Fasseur p.77

[103] Although Dutch law continues to speak of a "King", a Queen regnant also falls under this

uphold the Statute of the Kingdom and the Constitution in the exercise of the royal authority, as long as the King has not reached the age of 18 years. I swear that I will defend and save the independence and the territory of the Kingdom with all my might; that I will protect the freedom and the rights of all Dutch people and residents; that I will use all means available to me by law to maintain and improve the welfare, as a good and loyal regent must do. So help me, God almighty!"[104]

---

[104] https://wetten.overheid.nl/BWBR0006546/1994-05-14

2 August 1858 - The life of Emma of Waldeck and Pyrmont

Queen regent Emma RP-F-2007-112-13 via Rijksmuseum (public domain)

Emma of Waldeck and Pyrmont was born on 2 August 1858 as the daughter of Georg Viktor, Prince of Waldeck and Pyrmont, and Princess Helena of Nassau. She was their fourth daughter, and she would also have two younger sisters and a brother.

After her mother's death in 1888, her father remarried to Princess Louise of Schleswig-Holstein-Sonderburg-Glücksburg, and from that marriage, Emma also had a half-brother.

Emma and her sisters were raised by an English governess who taught her drawing and embroidery and French literature. She also had history lessons and learned to speak French, which would come in handy later on as her future husband did not speak German. The family also spent a lot of time travelling around Italy, England, Scandinavia and France.[105] Despite being from a small principality, the family was well-connected. Emma's aunt Sofia was Queen of Sweden and Norway. Another aunt was Duchess of Oldenburg and her uncle Adolphe would eventually become Grand Duke of Luxembourg.

Emma's daughter later wrote in her memoirs about her mother's youth, "As a young girl Mother enjoyed painting and drawing and had art lessons. I still possess a few of her old sketch-books. She always showed a lively interest in the arts and continued working with the etching-needle to an advanced age. She had a good feeling for line; her favourite subjects were flowers.

Her maturity at an early age is indicated by a letter I possess, written when she was about ten years old; it is a letter about practical matters, which my grandmother had told her to write.

"While she was living with her parents, she acquired an understanding of ordinary life which was very useful to her later on. She had an advantage over me in that respect; compelled to live in a cage by a convention which was inexorable in those days, I never

---

[105] Wilhelmina, de Jonge Koningin by Cees Fasseur p.43

had the opportunity to see 'normal life' as a child."[106]

About her education, she wrote, "She [Emma's mother] took a strong interest in the education of her children, who had their lessons at home. Owing to circumstances, my grandparents travelled frequently. They were always accompanied by a tutor and a governess. Quite often, the journeys lasted for several months and led through different countries. With all their travels, and with parents who regularly met and received interesting people, the children's human and intellectual development was really exceptionally favoured. Apart from their schooling by different tutors and governesses, the children also attended courses and did a great deal of independent reading. All were marked by this education and benefited from it later on. Meeting any one of them, one was invariably struck by their culture and general knowledge."[107]

On 7 January 1879, she married King William III of the Netherlands, who was 41 years older than she was. He had previously been married to Sophie of Württemberg, who had died in 1877. With Sophie, he had had three sons, of which one died young. At the time of his marriage to Emma, the younger William and Alexander were still alive. However, the younger William would die later that same year, deeply unhappy after being unable to marry the woman he loved. Both were vehemently against the marriage, and neither attended the wedding in Arolsen.

---

[106] Lonely but not alone p. 26-27

[107] Lonely but not alone p. 26

Emma gave birth to her only child, the future Queen Wilhelmina, on 31 August 1880. William had been present at the birth, encouraging Emma throughout the labour. William went to report his daughter's birth in person, giving her the names Wilhelmina Helena Paulina Maria, for several of her ancestors and three of Emma's sisters. Emma did not nurse Wilhelmina herself, as was tradition.

Wilhelmina was just three years old when her only surviving sibling, Alexander, also died. She was now the heiress presumptive to the throne.

Emma received praise from Queen Victoria during the wedding of her sister Helena to Queen Victoria's son Prince Leopold. Queen Victoria wrote to her eldest daughter, "The King of the Netherlands is as quiet and unobtrusive as possible; a totally altered man and totally owing to her. She is charming, so amiable, kind, friendly and cheerful.

"She would be very pretty were it not for her complexion which has suffered very much from the damp climate and is very red."[108] They visited the United Kingdom again the following year and they even brought along young Wilhelmina. As William's health deteriorated over the next years, Emma and Wilhelmina followed him around Europe to several spas. During these years, Emma taught her daughter to embroider. Wilhelmina also learned to ride horses from an early age.

---

[108] Dearest Mama edited by Roger Fulford p.118

In 1884, a law was approved that would make Emma regent if William died before Wilhelmina reached the age of 18 – which seemed very likely. When it became clear that Wilhelmina's father would likely not live to see her 18th birthday, her education was sped up. Her education focused on three languages, French, German and English but also included subjects just for her, like constitutional law and the organisation of the army. Emma was very involved in her daughter's education. William died on 23 November 1890 and Wilhelmina officially became Queen of the Netherlands with her mother as regent.

Emma was inexperienced, but she learned quickly, and she also began sharing her experiences with Wilhelmina early on. During her regency, support for the monarchy grew. Emma realised all too well that the monarchy needed the support of the people, and she actively sought contact with them.

 Emma chose to continue to follow precedent where she could and was always well-informed on matters. While William found it difficult to work with ministers, Emma was more compliant.

On 6 September 1898, Wilhelmina was inaugurated in the Nieuwe Kerk in Amsterdam. She later wrote, "While my mother was already in the church, I had to walk alone, all alone, with all those unknown gentlemen, from the palace to the church."[109] Emma had done her duty, but her job was not over yet. Especially during those early years, Wilhelmina often asked for her mother's advice.

---

[109] Wilhelmina, de Jonge Koningin by Cees Fasseur p.170

Also, a husband needed to be found for Wilhelmina. On 7 February 1901, she married Henry of Mecklenburg-Schwerin. Emma left Noordeinde Palace to the newlyweds and moved into the Lange Voorhout Palace nearby.

After two miscarriages and a stillbirth, Emma became a grandmother on 30 April 1909 with the birth of Princess Juliana. Juliana called her grandmother "Moemoem."[110] Emma was again named as a potential regent for her granddaughter Juliana, in case Wilhelmina died before Juliana's majority. After her regency ended, Emma often accompanied her daughter and son-in-law during public engagements. She also loved to travel and spent her time doing charity. She was especially devoted to fighting tuberculosis, the disease that had killed her sister Sophie and set up the first Dutch sanatorium for tuberculosis sufferers.

Emma and Wilhelmina corresponded to each other regularly though Wilhelmina would later destroy all of Emma's letters to her.[111] Emma had grown old rather quickly and had begun to suffer from several health problems. She remained as popular as ever and the 50th anniversary of her arrival in the Netherlands was celebrated in 1929. One of her final public appearances was in 1933, for Wilhelmina's 35th jubilee.

By early 1934, the Minister of Foreign Affairs described Emma as overtired, confused and in a bad physical condition.

---

[110] Wilhelmina, de Jonge Koningin by Cees Fasseur p.320

[111] Wilhelmina, Krijgshaftig in een vormeloze jas by Cees Fasseur p.29

He wrote, "She will only become enraged when she speaks of the Dutch National Socialism movement and Mussert. She hates them even more than the communists!"[112] Emma also had trouble sleeping and often suffered from toothache.

On 20 March 1934, Emma died after being ill for around a week from bronchitis that turned into pneumonia; she was 75 years old. Wilhelmina later wrote in her memoirs, "In March 1934, Juliana and I left her for a few days and went to The Loo for a little fresh air and a change of scene. Except for a slight cold, she seemed in good condition. We meant to stay away for only four or five days, a short winter holiday that I often took to escape from the obligations of life in town. Juliana always assisted Miss Schoch in her welfare work in Apeldoorn.

"This time, however, we soon received a telephone call from the doctor, who advised me to return immediately because Mother had suddenly fallen ill, and her condition gave rise to anxiety. We left at once. A few tense days followed. Juliana and I were with her at the Voorhout night and day and Henry paid several short visits, with the doctor's consent. On the 20th of March, God called her to him. On the 27th, we accompanied her to her last resting place in the vault of the Nieuwe Kerk in Delft, where she lies beside my father."[113]

"Since the end of her regency, she had devoted herself entirely to suffering humanity. The warmth of her interest and her intuitive

---

[112] Wilhelmina, Krijgshaftig in een vormeloze jas by Cees Fasseur p.88

[113] Lonely but not alone p. 139-140

understanding of the circumstances of those who suffered as well as of those who nursed them caused many a heart to rejoice in the course of the years. Mother's feelings went out to all, and she was a regular visitor in all classes of society. The news of her death caused general grief and regret among our people. We were particularly moved by the small tokens of love which were laid beside her bier, and perhaps even more by the expressions of those who came to as a last farewell."[114]

---

[114] Lonely but not alone p. 139-140

3 August 1914 - Neutrality and the First World War

Queen Wilhelmina during a military inspection RP-P-OB-106.088 via
Rijksmuseum (public domain)

On 28 June 1914, Archduke Franz Ferdinand of Austria and his wife
Sophie were assassinated in Sarajevo. The event has gone down in
history as the kickstarter of the Great War. However, at the time, not
all of Europe's royals were that concerned. Emperor Wilhelm II
continued to sail around Norway, and Queen Wilhelmina continued
to pose for a portrait with Henry and Juliana for Thérèse Schwartze
in the scorching heat.

On 28 July 1914, Austria declared war on Serbia and Russia began a
general mobilisation two days later. The Netherlands began
mobilisation on 31 July. On 1 August, Germany declared war on
Russia, followed by France and Belgium a few days later. Belgium
had declared their neutrality, which was violated, bringing England

in the mix - which then declared war on Germany on 4 August. However, the Dutch government was informed by Germany on 3 August that it would respect the neutrality of the Netherlands. Yet, the fighting in Belgium brought the war awfully close and both German and Belgian wounded soldiers were being treated in the Netherlands. The war violence also brought around 340,000 Belgian refugees to the Netherlands.

Of the neutrality, Wilhelmina wrote in her memoirs, "Neutrality in the sense in which it is used in international law does not simply mean that one stands aloof. It is a defined legal status which the neutral country has adopted, and the parties at war are obliged to respect its rights. The duties of neutrality are absolute and leave no room for human feelings. The situation can easily lead to tensions and struggles in the individual. At heart, man is never neutral, he always has a preference, sometimes without knowing it; and in a world-wide conflict, more than ever, his feelings are constantly involved, and his preference is reinforced."[115]

With the continued threat of the neutrality being violated, life for Wilhelmina changed dramatically. Festivities and ceremonies were cancelled, and shortages of things like coal became the norm. If Wilhelmina travelled at all, it was to places where disasters had taken place. In 1916, she visited areas that had been flooded. In May 1917, she visited the province of Drenthe after a peat fire which killed 16 people.

---

[115] Lonely but not alone p.96-97

She also made military inspections and was heavily involved in a committee that was meant to help with economic needs. She made several personal donations to the committee as well.

Wilhelmina later wrote in her memoirs, "The war suddenly imposed upon me the obligation to try and provide such leadership, or rather to let it proceed from me. I was fully aware that this could only be done once a new confidence in me had been created. A war makes special demands in this respect; the confidence that was sufficient in peacetime is no longer enough. Confidence was the word that echoed in me constantly; my thinking and acting were long dominated by the thought that I had to earn it. From morning till night, this idea never left me. At such moments one becomes conscious of the smallness of one's powers, and one realises acutely one's dependence on God's help."[116]

Wilhelmina also wrote, "My first duty was to be ready at all times. Everything was governed by it. This thought occupied me constantly and often worried me unnecessarily. I had to keep up this state of readiness till the end of the war, for on no account could I afford to be surprised by a major crisis at a moment when I was not in a state to take (make?) important decisions.[...] My love for the fatherland was like a consuming fire, and not only in me; it expressed itself in fierceness around me. It was only restricted by reflection and reason when the highest interests of people and the country demanded it.

---

[116] Lonely but not alone p.93

Anyone who threatened to damage these interests was my personal enemy. My thinking and my whole life was dominated by vigilance on their behalf."[117]

The personal German connections during the war were a bit more difficult. Both Queen Emma and Prince Henry were German and had extended family living in Germany. Queen Emma's half-brother Prince Wolrad was killed during the war in October 1914. On the other hand, Emma's sister Helena had married into the British Royal Family. Wilhelmina wrote in her memoirs, "Mother, who had taken up her residence at the Voorhout, spent the whole of the war in town so as to be immediately informed of the news and have daily contacts with us. She shared fully in my anxiety for the nation. She also had private worries concerning her relatives. One of her sisters lived in England, the widow of the Duke of Albany. Mother's thoughts often went out to her. Her other relatives lived in Germany. From a distance, she continued to give them her warm and loving sympathy."[118]

At the end of the war, the German monarchies came to an end. Queen Wilhelmina was most surprised to find the German Emperor looking for her help. On 10 November 1918, Wilhelm and his entourage appeared at a border post at Eijsden where he was denied entry. As Wilhelm paced around the train station of Eijsden, Wilhelmina was informed of the situation.

---

[117] Lonely but not alone p.99

[118] Lonely but not alone p.99-100

She later wrote, "I shall never forget the November morning at the Ruygenshoek when I was called very early with the news that the Kaiser had crossed our frontier in the province of Limburg. This communication from the government was soon followed by a telegram from the Kaiser himself, who tried to explain his action to me. I was utterly astonished; it was the very last thing I should have thought possible.[...] The Netherlands government assigned him a place of residence and demanded a promise that he would not leave it and would abstain from political activity. His abdication followed soon after."[119]

She added, "The flight and abdication of the Kaiser were followed by the abdication of the other German princes. Everything happened with incredible rapidity. Revolutionary elements and excited crowds demanded the abdication of their princes. The weaker ones gave in at once and left their lands precipitately; some other complied with greater dignity. Of course, they carried all the members of their families with them in their fall; none of them would be allowed to hold any public office. Even those who devoted the whole of their lives to the service of their peoples and who were held in the highest esteem were committed to the bitter fate of the outcast. In the meantime, the Allied victory had been gained and a cease-fire agreed upon. The armistice was then signed, and subsequently, the peace was dictated to Germany."[120]

---

[119] Lonely but not alone p.106-107

[120] Lonely but not alone p.107-108

5 August 1939 – The life of Princess Irene

Princess Irene with Prince Bernhard RP-F-00-7594 via Rijksmuseum (public domain)

Princess Irene of the Netherlands was born on 5 August 1939 as the second daughter of the future Queen Juliana and Prince Bernhard and she was thus a granddaughter of Queen Wilhelmina. Her eldest sister was the future Queen Beatrix, and her two younger sisters are Princess Margriet and the late Princess Christina.

Princess Irene was not yet one year old when the family was forced to flee to the United Kingdom, and her christening took place in the

Chapel Royal of Buckingham Palace on 31 May 1940 in the presence of both the Dutch and British royals. Queen Elizabeth the Queen Mother acted as one of her godparents. While Queen Wilhelmina set up a government in exile in London, it was decided that Juliana and her daughters should go to Canada for their safety. Princess Alice, Countess of Athlone, Wilhelmina's first cousin and her husband, who was the Governor-General of Canada, had offered to help. After all, England could be invaded as well. On 2 June 1940, Juliana, her daughters and several others boarded the HNLMS Sumatra, which was accompanied by the HNLMS Jacob van Heemskerck. Wilhelmina later wrote in her memoirs, "I gazed after the car as it drove off from Lydney Park - when and where would we meet again? Bernhard returned late in the evening, very unhappy at the prospect of their long separation. Several weeks passed before Juliana's first letter brought a ray of light for him and myself."[121] They arrived safely on 10 June 1940 and stayed at Government House at first. A month and a half later, they moved to a villa in Ottawa. Irene attended the Rockcliffe Park Public School before the family returned to the Netherlands in August 1945.

In 1948, Queen Wilhelmina abdicated, and Irene's mother became the new reigning Queen. Irene continued her education at the Werkplaats Kindergemeenschap. She also received private lessons before attending the Baarnsch Lyceum. She graduated in 1957 and went on to attend the University of Utrecht and Lausanne.

---

[121] Lonely but not alone p. 156

In 1963, she graduated with a degree in Spanish, and she became an official interpreter. While studying in Madrid, Irene met Carlos Hugo, Duke of Parma, who was the eldest son of the Carlist pretender to the Spanish throne. In the summer of 1963, Irene secretly converted to Roman Catholicism. Her subsequent engagement to Carlos Hugo caused a constitutional crisis, as she was second in line to the throne. Her mother tried to stop the marriage, but it was to no avail. On 9 February 1964, it was announced that Irene would give up her succession rights to marry Carlos Hugo.

On 29 April 1964, Princess Irene and Prince Carlos Hugo were married in Rome, and Irene was no longer a member of the Dutch Royal House. No one from her family attended the wedding in the Borghese Chapel at the Basilica di Santa Maria Maggiore in Rome. The ceremony was broadcast on TV, and the newlyweds were received by Pope Paul VI for a private audience. They went on to have four children together: Carlos, Duke of Parma (born 1970), Princess Margarita, Countess of Colorno (born 1972), Prince Jaime, Count of Bardi (born 1972, twin of Margarita) and Princess Carolina, Marchioness of Sala (born 1974). Their marriage ended in divorce in 1981. Irene and her children returned to the Netherlands, and her children later became part of the Dutch Nobility.

Princess Irene helped establish the NatuurCollege in the Netherlands, and she is the founder of NatureWise. She currently lives in Switzerland. Through her four children, she is currently a grandmother of ten.

6 August 1942 – Queen Wilhelmina addresses the United States Congress

Queen Wilhelmina addresses the United States Congress
RP-F-F01300 via Rijksmuseum (public domain)

On 6 August 1942, Queen Wilhelmina of the Netherlands addressed a joint session of the United States Senate and the House of Representatives - becoming the first reigning sovereign to do so. She said, "I stand here as the spokesman of my country, not only of those nine million of my compatriots in Europe but also of some seventy millions in Asia and in the Western Hemisphere, whom I know to be at one with me in the spirit. The Netherlands were, like the United States, like all the United Nations, a peace-loving country. At present, both in Europe and in Asia, that country is under enemy occupation. A cruel fate has overtaken its inhabitants.

Imagine what it means for a liberty-loving country to be in bondage, for a proud country to be subject to harsh alien rule. What would be the American answer if an invader tried to cover his wholesale systematic pillage with the firing squad, the concentration camp, and the abomination of the hostage practice? Having come by first-hand knowledge to know your national character better than ever, I doubt not that your answer would be: resistance, resistance until the end, resistance in every practicable shape or form."

[..]

United we stand, and united we will achieve victory."[122]

The New York Times reported of her speech, "Queen Wilhelmina didn't need to say or do anything more to endear her and her people to the Americans but her three days at Washington have had that effect. Busy days they were. She made a speech to Congress that was a model of clear statement, eloquent without rhetoric."[123]

During her time in the United States, she met President Roosevelt where she also ran into Märtha of Sweden, Crown Princess of Norway, and was briefly reunited with her daughter Juliana and her granddaughters. Queen Wilhelmina later wrote in her memoirs, "To me everything was new, and meeting the President and Mrs Roosevelt was an experience, although even at the first meeting with him I felt as if I was addressing an old friend, so cordial were his

---

[122]   https://www.dbnl.org/tekst/wilh001quee01_01/wilh001quee01_01_0012.php for the full text

[123] New York Times 8 August 1942

feelings for the Netherlands and for Juliana, Bernhard, the children and me."[124]

---

[124] Lonely but not alone p.181

31 August 1880 - The birth of Princess Wilhelmina

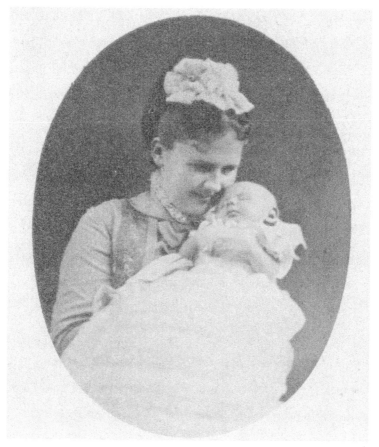

Emma and baby Wilhelmina RP-P-OB-105.717 via Rijksmuseum (public domain)

In early 1880 the new Queen Emma of the Netherlands realised she was expecting. By March, rumours were circulating around the country. In the evening of 30 August 1880, Emma went into labour at Noordeinde Palace and her husband was by her side throughout. A Princess was born the following day at six o'clock in the evening, much to (almost) everyone's joy. A 51-gun salute welcomed the Princess. King William showed no disappointment in the gender of his fourth child. She received the names Wilhelmina (a traditional Orange-Nassau name) Helena Pauline Maria (after three of Emma's sisters). The following day, William registered the birth himself and insisted on showing off the newborn Princess to the gentlemen in attendance, calling her "a beautiful child."[125]

At the time of her birth, the future Queen was third in the line of succession. At the time, the Netherlands operated on a semi-salic line of succession, and so, she was behind her elder half-brother Alexander (the only one of her three half-brothers still living) but also behind her great-uncle Prince Frederick. Prince Frederick died in 1881 without any surviving sons, followed by the unmarried Alexander in 1884, leaving Wilhelmina as her father's heir at the age of four.

Emma would not nurse the newborn Wilhelmina herself - she had two wetnurses, one at Noordeinde Palace and one the Loo Palace. And while her parents were overjoyed, several newspapers expressed their disappointment with headlines like, "It's only a girl!"[126] Only a son could have saved the royal house, with a girl the crown would inevitably pass to another house.

Nevertheless, congratulations began pouring in soon after the birth. Emma's sister Pauline wrote to William that little Wilhelmina would

---

[125] Wilhelmina, de Jonge Koningin by Cees Fasseur p. 60

[126] Wilhelmina, de Jonge Koningin by Cees Fasseur p. 61

be the joy of the rest of his life.[127]

The first years of her life appear to have been happy. She was appointed a governess named Cornelia Martina, Baroness van Heemstra, in 1882. She also had a carer named Marie Louise de Kock and a nanny named Julie Liotard, who also taught her French and so Wilhelmina was raised bilingual. Wilhelmina would remain the only child of her parents though she did not mind this, and she later wrote about the joy of having her parents all to herself.[128] When it became clear that she would become Queen sooner rather later, her education began in its earnest.

---

[127] Wilhelmina, de Jonge Koningin by Cees Fasseur p. 62

[128] Wilhelmina, de Jonge Koningin by Cees Fasseur p. 68

31 August 1885 - Happy Princess's day!

Princess Wilhelmina in 1885 RP-F-F17411 via Rijksmuseum (public domain)

These days the Netherlands celebrates King's Day but the traditional birthday celebrations for the monarch actually began (again) with Queen Wilhelmina, when she was just a Princess.

Princess Wilhelmina's father King William III was not quite the popular monarch he perhaps hoped to be, but his adorable four-year-old daughter and future Queen was very popular. A certain newspaper offered the suggestion that perhaps the birthday celebrations the country had once done for its first King, should now be done for the Princess. It also helped that her birthday was in August, while her father's birthday was in dreary February. They said it should be "a day where we put aside all grievances and feuds and to remember that we are countrymen and that a bond unites us all."[129]

People liked the idea and so the first Princess's day was celebrated on 31 August 1885 for Wilhelmina's fifth birthday. Princess Wilhelmina was paraded through the city of Utrecht, and in the following years, other cities followed. When Princess Wilhelmina's inherited the throne in 1890 at the age of 10, the day was renamed Queen's Day.

The festivities continued to grow, but Queen Wilhelmina rarely attended after she became an adult. During the Second World War, celebrations of Queen's Day were banned by the Germans. When Queen Wilhelmina abdicated in favour of her daughter Juliana, the Queen's Day celebrations were moved to Juliana's birthday on 30 April. The first celebration in April included a circus at the Amsterdam Olympic Stadium, but the family did not attend - preferring to stay at Soestdijk Palace where they received a floral tribute. When this tribute came to be televised in the 1950s, Queen's Day increasingly became the national holiday we know today.

---

[129] Wilhelmina, de Jonge Koningin by Cees Fasseur p. 72

SEPTEMBER

4 September 1948 – Queen Wilhelmina's abdication

Wilhelmina introduces her daughter as the new Queen RP-F-00-7438 via Rijksmuseum

When I studied history, I was particularly struck by the abdication of Emperor Charles V in 1555. I recognized the wisdom in it.[130]

Queen Wilhelmina's decision to abdicate certainly caused some raised eyebrows with her British cousins, who had been left reeling by the abdication of King Edward VIII in 1936.

When the future Queen Elizabeth II dedicated her entire life to her people at the age of 21, Queen Wilhelmina commented, "She has definitely settled better to the inevitable than me and has raised

---

[130] Lonely but not alone p.234

herself higher above it."[131]

Wilhelmina would not be the first Dutch monarch to abdicate - King William I abdicated in 1840 after wishing to marry Henriette d'Oultremont, his late wife's lady-in-waiting. Not only that, the Dutch Constitution expressly took abdication into account. Wilhelmina had begun toying with the idea of abdication in 1938, after a personal reign of 40 years. She had brought up the topic at a family dinner, but her daughter had not been up to it yet. Though the Second World War temporarily put all plans of abdication on hold, she continued to mention it occasionally in her letters to her daughter. By 1947, she was physically worn out and suffering from a heart condition which made it necessary for Princess Juliana to act as regent twice. Though her daughter tried to convince her to hold off her abdication until her golden jubilee, Wilhelmina dreaded celebrating another jubilee.

In her memoirs, Wilhelmina wrote, "It was only after the period of transition following the liberation that I felt justified in seriously considering the question of abdication. An incentive was provided by my daily duties, which were more numerous than before the war and left my spirit little or no time for relaxation, which did not help my fitness at moments when special demands were made of me."[132]

On 12 May 1948, Wilhelmina announced her intention to abdicate in a speech on the radio. The date had some significance as the date of

---

[131] Wilhelmina, Krijgshaftig in een vormeloze jas by Cees Fasseur p. 535

[132] Lonely but not alone p.235

her father's inauguration 99 years earlier. On 31 August 1948, a grand celebration took place in the Olympic Stadium of Amsterdam where she spoke the words, "I have fought the good fight."[133] She would officially abdicate on 4 September 1948, 50 years and four days since the start of her personal reign. She signed her abdication in the Royal Palace of Amsterdam which was co-signed by her daughter and son-in-law. She later wrote, "When we entered we found a somewhat subdued atmosphere, which was however soon improved by my happy and cheerful manner. How numerous were and are my reasons for gratitude, in the first place, my confidence in Juliana's warm feelings for the people we both love so much and in her devotion to the task that was awaiting her and her ability which she had proved on various occasions. Then also the fact that my office was transferred to her during my lifetime and that I might have the opportunity to see something of her reign. Really, there was no room for sadness in my heart."[134]

Then Wilhelmina - who had now reverted back to the title and style of Her Royal Highness Princess Wilhelmina - took her daughter to the balcony of the palace to introduce her as the new Queen. She said, "I am honoured to inform you myself that I just signed my abdication in favour of my daughter Queen Juliana. I thank you all for the trust you have placed in me for the last fifty years. I thank you for the affection with which you have surrounded me every

---

[133] Wilhelmina, Krijgshaftig in een vormeloze jas by Cees Fasseur p. 538

[134] Lonely but not alone p.237

time. I look to the future with confidence with my darling only child in charge. God be with you and the Queen. And I am happy to say with all of you, long live our Queen! Huzzah!"

Princess Wilhelmina left the palace through the back door later that day.

6 September 1898 - The inauguration of Queen Wilhelmina

Queen Wilhelmina walks to the church RP-F-F03183 via Rijksmuseum (public domain)

Just six days after her 18th birthday, Queen Wilhelmina of the Netherlands walked from the Royal Palace in Amsterdam to the adjacent Nieuwe Kerk to have her inauguration as Queen of the Netherlands. She had succeeded her father as a girl of 10, and for eight years, her mother had served as regent - now her personal reign would begin. She wore the same mantle her grandfather King William II had worn in 1840.

Before swearing an oath to the Dutch Constitution, she held a short speech in which she said, "I believe it to be a great privilege that it is my task and duty in life to devote all my strength to the wellbeing and growth of the Fatherland so precious to me. I make the words of my beloved father my own, "Orange can never, yes never, do enough for the Netherlands."[135] Her mother sat slightly behind her on the podium.

The oath goes as follows:

"I swear to the people of the Kingdom that I will maintain and uphold the Statute of the Kingdom and the Constitution. I swear that I will defend and maintain the independence and the lands of the Kingdom with all my might, that I will protect the freedoms and the rights of the Dutch citizens and inhabitants, and to use all means available to me by law for the maintenance and improvement of the welfare, like a good and loyal King is obligated to do. So help me, God Almighty!"[136]

Following her own oath, all of the present members of the States-General swore their allegiance to her.

She later wrote in her memoirs of the moment she walked into the church all alone, "A feeling of emptiness and complete loneliness came over me."[137] Prime Minister Pierson was deeply touched by the inauguration and wrote, "The inauguration was so very impressive that it touched all of our souls."[138]

Exactly 50 years later, Queen Wilhelmina's only surviving child Juliana was inaugurated as Queen of the Netherlands.

---

[135] https://historiek.net/de-inhuldiging-van-koningin-wilhelmina-1898/70940/

[136] https://www.parlement.com/id/vicngdvdngpw/inhuldiging_koning

[137] Lonely but not alone p.58

[138] Wilhelmina, de Jonge Koningin by Cees Fasseur p. 171

15 September 1843 - The short life of Prince Maurice

Prince Maurice RP-P-OB-105.753 via Rijksmuseum (public domain)

Queen Wilhelmina of the Netherlands would never know any of elder half-brothers. The first of them to die was Prince Maurice, whose life was cut short by disease.

Prince Maurice was born on 15 September 1843 in The Hague as the second son of the future King William III of the Netherlands and his first wife, Sophie of Württemberg. William delivered the news to his father King William II in person and called himself, "the happiest man in the world."[139] He looked to be stronger and bigger than his elder brother - another William - but he soon turned out to be rather sickly. Maurice was a calm and friendly child, and his mother lived in constant worry over his delicate health. This was in no way helped by the death of young Prince Frederick, the ten-year-old son of her husband's uncle - also named Frederick- and Louise of Prussia. Sophie wrote, "I am so sad, so sad; if something like that happened to me, by God, I hope I will also die. Of course, I am receiving no one. Our mourning will last for weeks. The funeral is next Wednesday or Thursday. I keep walking to my children, to see, to hear, to feel that they are alive."[140]

The governor of Maurice's elder brother wrote of the two brothers in 1849, "While W. is always sullen, rude and unkind, M., on the other hand, is politeness and kindness itself. His health is very delicate, as a consequence of bad living. The conclusion must be that both their educations have been miserable, though W.'s character has been damaged the most."[141]

In May 1850, Maurice became ill yet again. Sophie had lost all faith in the court doctor Everard and called for another doctor, named Ter Winkel. He diagnosed an "unclean stomach" and administered

---

[139] Koning Willem III by Dik van der Meulen p.153

[140] Koning Willem III by Dik van der Meulen p.154

[141] Koning Willem III by Dik van der Meulen p.297

several medications, including musk. Maurice's father had no faith in the medicines or the doctor. Doctor Everard was eventually called, and he diagnosed a "nervous illness with the beginnings of meningitis." Ter Winkel laughed the diagnosis away and told Sophie that there was no danger whatsoever. Sophie's husband angrily told Ter Winkel to leave at once. As Maurice's condition deteriorated, William called for two more doctors, Van Bylandt and Vinkhuyzen. It was too late for young Maurice. Sophie often dragged young William to his brother's bed, against the will of the doctors and her husband. On 4 June, around 5 in the afternoon, she had taken him to see his brother once more, but he was taken away by his governor. Despite his illness, Maurice recognised the governor and said, "Hello, sir" in a hoarse voice. Just 15 minutes later, they learned that Maurice had passed away. Sophie would never forgive herself for bringing in Ter Winkel, and her friend Lady Malet admitted that Sophie was never happy again. She wrote, "Always running from herself. A never-ending torture."[142]

Maurice was just six years old when he died. On 10 June 1850, he was interred in the royal crypt in Delft.

---

[142] Koning Willem III by Dik van der Meulen p.307

20 September 1898 – Queen Wilhelmina's first speech from the throne

The Knight's Hall RP-F-F19674 via Rijksmuseum (public domain)

Queen Wilhelmina of the Netherlands' first official act after all the inauguration celebrations was her speech from the throne on Prinsjesdag (Literal translation: Little Prince's Day) on 20 September 1898. During Queen Wilhelmina's minority, her mother had handled the speech from the throne. Queen Wilhelmina had attended the 1897 speech from the throne with her mother, and after the end of her regency, Queen Emma still often joined her daughter for the speech.

Prinsjesdag is the day on which the reigning monarch addresses a joint session of the Dutch Senate and House of Representatives to set out the main government policies for the coming parliamentary session. The assembly of the States-General usually takes places in the Ridderzaal (Knight's Hall) though during Queen Wilhelmina's early reign it was held in the assembly room of the House of Representatives as the Ridderzaal was being renovated.

Queen Wilhelmina had received a Golden Coach for her inauguration, and although this became the traditional coach to use during Prinsjesdag later (not currently, as it's being renovated), it was first used for Prinsjesdag in 1903. Before this, Queen Wilhelmina used the Glass Coach. Queen Wilhelmina missed just four years in total. In 1908 and 1909, she was pregnant and subsequently gave birth to Princess Juliana and was thus absent. In 1911, she was annoyed with the Speaker of the House of Representatives as he did not withdraw from his post as she wished him to do and subsequently refused to hold the speech. She was ill in 1947. If the monarch is not available, the speech is held by a member of a commission on behalf of the monarch.

Queen Wilhelmina and Queen Emma travelled together in the Glass Coach through The Hague for her first Prinsjesdag. To give as many people as possible the chance to see them, the way back was a bit longer. While Queen Emma was dressed in black velvet, Queen Wilhelmina wore a white satin dress with silver embroidery. She also wore the ribbon of the Order of the Netherlands Lion. She also wore a small hat with three curled feathers. When her six-minute speech was over, the attendees cheered, "Long live the Queen!" and "Long live the Queen Mother!" Once the two Queens were back at Noordeinde Palace, they showed themselves in the window to the public.[143]

---

[143] https://shop.vorsten.nl/vorstenhuizen/nederland-vorstenhuizen/paul-rem-wilhelminas-eerste-prinsjesdag/

25 September 1890 – Princess Wilhelmina sees her father for the last time

Emma, William and Emma RP-P-OB-105.706 via Rijksmuseum (public domain)

From 1889, the health of Wilhelmina's father King William III of the Netherlands deteriorated quickly. On 12 May 1889, he celebrated the 40th anniversary of his inauguration in quite reasonable health. However, by August he suffered a setback, supposedly some kind of stroke. From then on, he stayed put at The Loo Palace in Apeldoorn. From the summer of 1890, his moods went from calm in the morning to aggressive later in the day. He was often up during the night and would wake up servants, complaining to them of hammering and knocking that appeared to exist only in his mind. He also began to suffer from excruciating headaches. Wilhelmina celebrated her 10th birthday on 31 August 1890 but from then on things moved quickly. He apparently suffered another stroke which, "shocked the brains of His Majesty so deeply, that His Majesty was completely out of it."[144]

On 25 September 1890, he saw Wilhelmina for the very last time. The long months of his illness affected the young Wilhelmina very much. She wrote in her memoirs, "Although during the last few months his suffering was such that I could no longer visit him, this period left a deep mark on my life. The atmosphere at The Loo was dominated by his illness. Everything became strained. When his illness was at its worst Mother spent all her time at his bedside, and I hardly saw her. How much it means to a child when her Mother disappears out of her life, and for such a long time! The last night she did not come to bed at all - I had been sleeping in her room for some time - and that night I felt that something terrible was happening upstairs in Father's room. People tried to hide it from me, but yet I knew what that terrible thing was."[145]

The 10-year-old Princess Wilhelmina would soon become the Netherlands' first Queen regnant.

---

[144] Koning Willem III by Dik van der Meulen p.638

[145] Lonely but not alone p.23

OCTOBER

7 October 1948 – Princess Wilhelmina receives the Military Order of William

Wilhelmina wearing the insignia of the Military Order of William
NG-1972-11-196 via Rijksmuseum (public domain)

The Military Order of William is the highest honour of the Kingdom of the Netherlands and was named for St. William of Gellone, the very first Prince of Orange. It was founded in 1815 by King William I of the Netherlands for bravery on the battlefield and as a decoration for senior military officers.

It is open to everyone, regardless of rank, and extends to foreigners as well. It is currently very rarely awarded. Its motto is "For Bravery, Leadership and Loyalty."

After the Second World War, it was decided that the Military Order of William could also be granted to civilians for heroics in the resistance. One of the first acts of Queen Juliana as sovereign was to sign the order to grant her mother, then known as Princess Wilhelmina, the Grand Cross of the Military Order of William. The official ceremony took place in Arnhem on 7 October 1948, and Queen Juliana praised her mother as "Mother of the Fatherland", who had strengthened the will of the people in the days of the occupation during the Second World War.[146]

Several others were also awarded the Military Order of William in a lower class. The four classes are Knight Grand Cross, Commander, Knight 3rd Class and Knight 4th Class. Upon acceptance, an oath is spoken: "I swear that I shall conduct myself as a faithful and valiant Knight, to stand ever ready to defend King and Country with my Life, and with all my Powers to always strive to be worthy of this Distinction, which the King has bestowed upon me. So help me, God almighty."

Wilhelmina learned that she would be awarded the order during Juliana's speech at her inauguration. She wrote in her memoirs, "When all were seated, Juliana delivered her speech, to which I listened in breathless tension. I have read it many times since. What she said to me came so directly from the heart that I felt a little less embarrassed and unhappy than I should have done if the words had come from another.

---

[146]   https://www.koninklijkeverzamelingen.nl/collectie-online/detail/b676415b-3d6e-5ecc-bfa5-0bac1e850b2e

This also applied to my appointment as a knight first class of the Military Order of William, which came as a complete surprise. I regard this as a tribute to all my brave fellow-fighters during the war."[147]

As of 2020, there are four living knights.

---

[147] Lonely but not alone p.238

12 October 1880 – Princess Wilhelmina's baptism

Princess Wilhelmina RP-P-OB-106.142 via Rijksmuseum (public domain)

In early 1880 the new Queen Emma of the Netherlands realised she was expecting. By March, rumours were circulating around the country. In the evening of 30 August 1880, Emma went into labour at Noordeinde Palace and her husband was by her side throughout. A Princess was born the following day at six o'clock in the evening, much to (almost) everyone's joy. A 51-gun salute welcomed the Princess. King William showed no disappointment in the gender of his fourth child. She received the names Wilhelmina (a traditional Orange-Nassau name) Helena Pauline Maria (after three of Emma's sisters). She was initially known as Pauline, though her parents later switched to Wilhelmina. The following day, William registered the birth himself and insisted on showing off the newborn Princess to the gentlemen in attendance, calling her "a beautiful child."[148]

At the time of her birth, the future Queen was third in the line of succession. At the time, the Netherlands operated on a semi-salic line of succession, and so, she was behind her elder half-brother Alexander (the only one of her three half-brothers still living) but also behind her great-uncle Prince Frederick. Prince Frederick died in 1881 without any surviving sons, followed by the unmarried Alexander in 1884, leaving Wilhelmina as her father's heir at the age of four.

The baptism of the infant Princess took place on 12 October 1880 in the reformed Willemskerk in The Hague with all the royal ceremony they could muster. There was a horsedrawn carriage with six horses, three lackeys by the door and two gentlemen who carried the train of the satin baptismal gown. The baptismal gown would be worn by Princess Juliana in 1909, Princess Beatrix in 1938, Prince Willem-Alexander in 1967 and Princess Catharina-Amalia in 2004.

Pastor Van Koetsveld held the sermon with the words, "Children are the blossom of life." For the first time in many years, it was the mother herself who held Wilhelmina as she was baptised. Most of the extended family was present, except for Emma's mother who was not well and Wilhelmina's half-brother Alexander.

---

[148] Wilhelmina, de Jonge Koningin by Cees Fasseur p. 60

12 October 1900 - The engagement of Henry and Wilhelmina

Wilhelmina and Henry RP-F-1928-22 via Rijksmuseum (public domain)

Emperor Wilhelm wasn't the only who believed that only a German Prince would do for the young Queen Wilhelmina; her mother wanted it too.

But while Emperor Wilhelm preferred Frederick William of Prussia, who also happened to be a quarter Dutch as the grandson of Princess

Marianne of the Netherlands (daughter of King William I), Emma preferred the two youngest sons of Frederick Francis II, Grand Duke of Mecklenburg-Schwerin - Adolf Frederick and Henry. Their sister-in-law Princess Elisabeth Sybille of Saxe-Weimar-Eisenach - married to their elder brother Duke Johann Albrecht of Mecklenburg-Schwerin - was in contact with Queen Emma. In 1896, she and her husband were invited to The Loo Palace and Soestdijk Palace. The names of her husband's half-brothers must have been mentioned during this time.

Wilhelmina had met both brothers for the first time in 1892 when she was just 12 years old. The meeting had happened at her aunt Sophie's golden wedding anniversary celebrations in Weimar but was unlikely to have made a lasting impression on the young Queen. A second meeting with Henry planned for 1898 had to be cancelled because Wilhelmina had been ill. It wasn't until May 1900, another meeting was arranged.

From 8 May until 5 June, the two Queens were going to visit Schwarzburg, staying in the Weisser Hirsch hotel. Wilhelmina could take long walks without being seen, and she could also meet potential suitors.

As Schwarzburg was also the home of Henry's maternal family, and he happened to be visiting his grandmother, she met Henry first. In return, the two Queens also visited Schloss Schwarzburg and received an invitation for a walk and picnic from Henry's unmarried aunt Thekla.

Apparently, the picnic and walk were so much fun that Wilhelmina wondered, "if a walk hand in hand through life was to be recommended."[149]

It should be noted that Henry's brother Adolf never did show his face in Schwarzburg, but the Emperor's candidate Frederick William did show his face. Wilhelmina thought he had a baby-face (they were actually only a few weeks apart in age) and quickly vetoed him. This left only Henry. Wilhelmina later wrote in her memoirs, "When he had left, a few days later, we had dinner with Grandmother Schwarzburg. I missed him very much, although it was a pleasant evening."[150]

Henry was silent for a long time after the trip to Schwarzburg and he did not contact Wilhelmina again until October. They became officially engaged on 12 October 1900. After lunch, Wilhelmina and Henry were finally left alone for a few moments. Just ten minutes later, the two emerged as an engaged couple. She later wrote in her memoirs, "The die was cast. What a relief that always is on these occasions!"[151]

Wilhelmina wrote to her former governess, "Oh Darling, you cannot even faintly imagine how franticly happy I am and how much joy, and sunshine has come upon my path."[152]

---

[149] Wilhelmina de jonge Koningin by Cees Fasseur p.215

[150] Lonely but not alone p.6

[151] Lonely but not alone p.63

[152] Darling Queen, Dear old bones edited by Emerentia van Heuven-van Nes p. 271

16 October 1900 - The announcement of the engagement between Wilhelmina and Henry

With their engagement having just taken place four days previously, Queen Wilhelmina and Henry announced their engagement on 16 October 1900 with a proclamation.

"To my people!

It is a need to me, to the Dutch people, of whose lively interest in the happiness of me and my House I am so deeply convinced, to inform you personally of my engagement with His Highness, Duke Henry of Mecklenburg-Schwerin.

May this event, with God's blessing, benefit the wellbeing of our country and its possessions and colonies in East and West. [..]

Done at The Loo Palace, on this day 16 October 1900 - Wilhelmina."

A delighted Wilhelmina wrote to her former governess Miss Winter, "Oh darling, you cannot even faintly imagine how frantically happy I am and how much joy, and sunshine has come upon my path."[153]

After heavy negotiations concerning his income, his status and titles, the two were married on 7 February 1901. Henry became known as Prince Hendrik in the Netherlands, and he became Prince Consort.

---

[153] Darling Queen, Dear old bones edited by Emerentia van Heuven-van Nes p. 271

He was also awarded the style of "Royal Highness." Henry's initial reception in the Netherlands had been somewhat lukewarm, but his popularity grew over time. One of the defining moments for this came in 1907 when the Berlin ferry - which served the Harwich/Hook of Holland route - broke in two and sank. Henry arrived the following day to help with the recovery of the bodies, but they also found a handful of survivors on the floating stern. There had been around 144 passengers on board. Once the survivors had been brought to safety, Henry helped to care for the victims and even poured them coffee or cognac. His easy-going nature also made him popular amongst the palace servants.

Though initially a happy match, Wilhelmina and Henry would grow apart over the years. She would suffer several miscarriages and a stillbirth before finally giving birth to a healthy baby girl named Juliana in 1909. She was his pride and joy until the day he died, and they always remained on good terms, despite the wavering relationship between Henry and Wilhelmina.

20 October 1912 - A fifth miscarriage

With Wilhelmina's marriage to Henry of Mecklenburg-Schwerin on 7 February 1901, she and her mother both fervently prayed for healthy children to continue their line. Tragically, Wilhelmina would go on to suffer five miscarriages and only one healthy child was born to Wilhelmina and Henry.

Though the relief at the birth of Princess Juliana in 1909 was great, she would remain an only child to her regret but also to the regret of Wilhelmina and Henry. The fifth and final miscarriage happened at Noordeinde Palace on 20 October 1912. Kouwer, the gynaecologist who had stood by Wilhelmina through the many miscarriages, was summoned but there was nothing more he could do. Newspapers reported a "minor indisposition of the Queen" that "foiled the hope that had been held briefly."[154]

Wilhelmina herself found solace in her faith as she always did. Without specifically referencing her miscarriages, she wrote in her memoirs, "My faith and love for Christ were subjected to many tests in the course of my life. The first test was the decisive one. In difficult circumstances, I was confronted with an inescapable choice: to remain true to Him at a time when it demanded a sacrifice, or to give in to temptation, even for only a moment.

"I recognised clearly that it would be shameful to follow Him in

---

[154] De grondwet 24-10-1912

prosperity and to deny Him in adversity; to forget one's vow when it demanded self-abnegation, to argue; that is not how I meant my promise to follow Him. To forsake this loyalty, the highest and best thing in us - I could not even bear to think of what one would be after such an irreparable rupture. After a struggle, I made the sacrifice and chose to do Christ's will."[155]

---

[155] Lonely but not alone p. 82

NOVEMBER

9 November 1901 – The first miscarriage

With Wilhelmina's marriage to Henry of Mecklenburg-Schwerin on 7 February 1901, she and her mother both fervently prayed for healthy children to continue their line. Tragically, Wilhelmina would go on to suffer five miscarriages and only one healthy child was born to Wilhelmina and Henry.

At the end of August 1901, the first signs of pregnancy were showing, and Queen Wilhelmina wrote to her mother, "Don't be frightened when you read in the papers tomorrow that I had to keep to my bed due to stomach issues. You cannot tell anyone, anyone, the true reason, please. I am still very uncertain."[156] It turned out to be a false alarm.

But she was a lot more certain a few months later. She reported to her mother in early November, "Now the newspapers are reporting that I am unwell, very interesting."[157] Just a week later, Wilhelmina suffered her first miscarriage. No clear cause could be identified, and both Henry and Emma rushed to be by Wilhelmina's side. Doctors informed Wilhelmina that she should rest for at least four weeks but that there was no reason to fear that she would not become pregnant again.

Nevertheless, Wilhelmina was racked with guilt. She wrote to her

[156] Wilhelmina, de Jonge Koningin by Cees Fasseur p. 261

[157] Wilhelmina, de Jonge Koningin by Cees Fasseur p. 261

mother, "You don't know how sorry I was to have hurt you, you don't know, and I think I am very, very ugly. It was all my own evil fault. I won't write about it any more, loopholes and 'buts' won't make it any better. I just wanted to say that it really messed with my head. Really, little mother, I am saddened by it."[158]

Although Queen Wilhelmina made a full recovery, Christmas at court was quite austere that year.

The following year, Wilhelmina fell ill with typhoid fever and shortly after that, on 4 May 1902, gave birth to a premature stillborn son. On 23 July 1906, a third miscarriage followed. A fourth pregnancy ended in the birth of the future Queen Juliana on 30 April 1909. A fourth miscarriage followed on 23 January 1912. A fifth and final miscarriage took place on 20 October 1912. The cause of the miscarriages has not been identified, and we'll probably never know for sure.

---

[158] Wilhelmina, de Jonge Koningin by Cees Fasseur p. 263

23 November 1890 – Becoming Queen

Emma and Wilhelmina in mourning RP-F-1928-19 via Rijksmuseum (public domain)

Princess Wilhelmina has last seen her father on 25 September 1890. She wrote in her memoirs, "Although during the last few months his suffering was such that I could no longer visit him, this period left a deep mark on my life. The atmosphere at The Loo was dominated by his illness. Everything became strained. When his illness was at its worst Mother spent all her time at his bedside, and I hardly saw her. How much it means to a child when her Mother disappears out of her life, and for such a long time! The last night she did not come to bed at all - I had been sleeping in her room for some time - and that night I felt that something terrible was happening upstairs in Father's room. People tried to hide it from me, but yet I knew what that terrible thing was."[159]

On 20 November, Wilhelmina's mother Emma left behind her dying husband to swear the oath of regency in her husband's name in The Hague. She told the States-General, "In these serious days, where the King's condition fills us all with sadness, I will act as regent of the Kingdom. The King, my beloved and honoured consort, has given me the highest example of royal duty and working in the interested of the Country and the People, which has always set the House of Orange apart. I consider it my duty to follow his example. May God ease the suffering of our King and take the Netherlands under His holy wing."[160]

When Emma returned to the Loo Palace later that day, his condition had deteriorated considerably. He had grown restless, and his kidneys were failing. The following night, he suddenly stood up and threw off the covers. His feet were swollen so he could not walk, and his servant told him to get back into bed, upon which the King

---

[159] Lonely but not alone p.23

[160] Koning Willem III by Dik van der Meulen p.638

asked, "Who gives the orders here, you or me?" They were his last words.

William on his deathbed RP-P-OB-106.263 via Rijksmuseum (public domain)

William fell back to sleep and only occasionally awoke during the following two days, unable to recognise anyone. He died on 23 November 1890, at 5.45 in the morning. His funeral took place on 4 December - the date was specifically chosen by Emma so that the Dutch people could still celebrate St. Nicholas' eve.

On 8 December, Emma once again took the oath of the regency - this time in her daughter's name. The 10-year-old Princess Wilhelmina had become the Netherlands' first Queen regnant.

23 November 1890 – The loss of Luxembourg

The Grand Ducal Palace in Luxembourg RP-F-F02165 via Rijksmuseum (public domain)

The Grand Duchy of Luxembourg had been a province of the Kingdom of the Netherlands since its foundation in 1815 before becoming independent but remaining in personal union with the Kingdom following the Treaty of London of 1839. It consisted of the territory of the duchy of Luxembourg, which had been a state of the Holy Roman Empire. Subsequently, the monarchs of the Netherlands were also Grand Dukes of Luxembourg.

The succession in Luxembourg was dictated by the Nassau family pact of 1793 and although King William III had attempted to change it to secure Luxembourg for Wilhelmina, it was Emma who convinced him not to do it. The Nassau family pact stipulated that Luxembourg would go from the Ottonian branch to the Walramian branch of the Nassau family if the Ottonian branch died out in the male line - which it did with King William III's death in 1890. The head of the Walramian branch of the family was Adolphe, Duke of Nassau - whose lands had been annexed by Prussia in 1866. Adolphe also happened to be Queen Emma's uncle - being her mother's elder half-brother. Emma convinced William that it would not be chivalrous towards their less fortunate family to change the pact now.[161]

On 23 November 1890, upon the death of King William III, his daughter Wilhelmina succeeded him as Queen of the Netherlands while Adolphe became Grand Duke of Luxembourg.

In any case, Adolphe's son William did not have any sons of his own and he named his elder daughter Marie-Adélaïde as heiress presumptive in 1907. This too had been arranged for in the Nassau family pact in the case both lines died out without male heirs and thus fulfilled this clause. The current Grand Duke of Luxembourg is the grandson of Marie-Adélaïde's sister Charlotte, who succeeded her in 1919.

Luxembourg introduced absolute primogeniture - where the elder child succeeds regardless of gender - in 2011.

---

[161] Wilhelmina, de jonge Koningin by Cees Fasseur p.105

28 November 1962 - The death of Princess Wilhelmina

Wilhelmina RP-F-F02165 via Rijksmuseum (public domain)

By 1947, Queen Wilhelmina was physically worn out and suffering from a heart condition which made it necessary for Princess Juliana to act as regent twice. Though her daughter tried to convince her to hold off her abdication until her golden jubilee, Wilhelmina dreaded celebrating another jubilee. In her memoirs, Wilhelmina wrote, "It was only after the period of transition following the liberation that I felt justified in seriously considering the question of abdication. An incentive was provided by my daily duties, which were more numerous than before the war and left my spirit little or no time for relaxation, which did not help my fitness at moments when special demands were made of me."[162] Queen Wilhelmina abdicated in favour of her only child Juliana on 4 September 1948 and reverted to the title of Princess Wilhelmina.

After her abdication, Princess Wilhelmina spent a lot of time on religion, and she felt relieved to no longer have the burden of government on her shoulders. She remained in daily contact with her daughter but rarely appeared in public. She retreated to the Loo Palace, where she would eventually inhabit just a few small rooms in the staff quarters. She took up painting again and often went out riding on the Veluwe. She also liked to ride her bicycle, and her bicycle always stood ready and waiting for at the back entrance of the Palace. She also set about writing her memoirs, which were also translated in English. Tragically, she also burned a lot of correspondence, like letters from her mother. She wrote, "It was very necessary to burn a lot."[163] Wilhelmina also took up travelling - visiting Switzerland, the United Kingdom and Norway in 1951, France in 1953, and Norway again in 1953, 1954 and 1955.

---

[162] Lonely but not alone p.235

[163] Wilhelmina, Krijgshaftig in een vormeloze jas by Cees Fasseur p.548

She spent her 80th birthday in 1960 in private at the Loo Palace, though over 400 telegrams were delivered to congratulate her on her birthday. In the autumn of 1962, she began having issues with her heart again and wrote to her first cousin Princess Alice, Countess of Athlone "Since a few weeks I am struggling hard against my old complaint."[164] But Wilhelmina was not afraid.

Wilhelmina remained conscious throughout her final days. She died just before 1 A.M. on 28 November 1962. A press release stated, "In the last few weeks signs appeared of a heart disease that had to be considered as being very serious in view of her age. Notwithstanding a slight improvement, her illness took a turn for the worse yesterday. The gradual deterioration of her general state of health, which was already bad, was speeded [sic] up."[165]

Queen Juliana announced her mother's death with the words, "It has pleased God to call my dear mother to him. She expired peacefully today. I am convinced that the Dutch people will share the great gratitude with me and mine that we feel has been given to us by this life."[166]

---

[164] Wilhelmina, Krijgshaftig in een vormeloze jas by Cees Fasseur p.564

[165] The New York Times - 28 November 1962

[166] Het Parool - 29-11-1962

DECEMBER

8 December 1890 - Queen Emma takes the regency oath

Emma takes the oath RP-P-OB-105.723 via Rijksmuseum (public domain)

On 20 November 1890, Wilhelmina's mother Emma left behind her dying husband, King William III of the Netherlands, to swear the oath of regency in her husband's name in The Hague. She told the States-General, "In these serious days, where the King's condition fills us all with sadness, I will act as regent of the Kingdom. The King, my beloved and honoured consort, has given me the highest example of royal duty and working in the interested of the Country and the People, which has always set the House of Orange apart. I consider it my duty to follow his example. May God ease the suffering of our King and take the Netherlands under His holy wing."[167]

He died just a few days later, and on 8 December, Queen Emma was back to swear the oath again - now in the name of the new sovereign; her 10-year-old daughter Queen Wilhelmina. In addition to the regency oath, she also took a separate oath as the guardian of the Queen. The oath stated, "I swear loyalty to the King; I solemnly swear to fulfil all the duties the guardianship places upon me and to focus especially on instilling in the King an attachment to the Constitution and a love for his people. So help me, God Almighty."[168]

---

[167] Koning Willem III by Dik van der Meulen p.638

[168] Article 34 of the 1887 Constitution

8 December 1962 – A white funeral

The white hearse RP-F-F01390 via Rijksmuseum (public domain)

Princess Wilhelmina had died on 28 November 1962 at 1 in the morning in a small staff apartment at her beloved Loo Palace. As early as 1919, Wilhelmina had settled on a so-called "white funeral." Her husband had also requested a white funeral, and she observed his wishes upon his death in 1934. In her memoirs, Wilhelmina wrote, "Long before he died my husband and I had discussed the meaning of death and the eternal Life that follows it. We both had the certainty of faith that death is the beginning of Life, and therefore had promised each other that we would have white funerals. This agreement was now observed. Hendrik's white funeral, as his last gesture to the nation, made a profound impression and set many people thinking.[169]

Queen Juliana and her daughters in white RP-F-F01392 via Rijksmuseum (public domain)

The hearse, church and the mourning clothes should be white, while the coffin should be covered with the Dutch flag and an open bible. She refused to have any regalia placed on the coffin.

---

[169] Lonely but not alone p.141

She wanted to have people from all layers of the Dutch society to be present at the funeral as well as deserving military personnel of all ranks. She also did not want to be embalmed.

For several days, her body lay in state in the court chapel of the Loo Palace as people paid their respects. On the evening of 4 December, her body was transferred to the Lange Voorhout Palace in The Hague, which had been the home of her mother, Queen Emma. As her body left the Loo Palace, the anthem "Mein Waldeck" was played.

At the Lange Voorhout Palace, people paid their respects as well. Just one wreath was on top of the coffin as it was taken to the Nieuwe Kerk in Delft for burial in the royal crypt - it was from the Dutch resistance. Along the route was an honour guard of 9,000 soldiers. There were no royal regalia as per her wish, but the insignia of the Military Order of William she had been so proud of receiving were there. She did not want foreign representatives to be there, but several members of the extended family were there, such as her first cousin Princess Alice, Countess of Athlone and the Wied family.

In the church were almost 3,000 people who listened to the service held in Dutch by court preacher Berkel and in French by preacher Forget.

In the sermon, they addressed the role of the Father of the Fatherland - William of Orange - and also included her mother Emma and her husband Henry and the situation during the Second World War.[170]

---

[170] Wilhelmina, Krijgshaftig in een vormeloze jas by Cees Fasseur p.566

Her coffin was placed in the royal crypt next to her husband Henry and her parents King William III and Queen Emma.

Bibliography

Alexander, de vergeten kroonprins by Fred J. Lammers Beloved &
Darling Child edited by Agatha Ramm

Beloved Mama edited by Roger Fulford

Darling Queen, Dear old bones edited by Emerentia van Heuven-van
Nes

Daughter of Empire: My Life as a Mountbatten by Pamela Hicks

De Oranjes in de Tweede Wereldoorlog by Carel Brendel

Hendrik Prins der Nederlanden by J.A. de Jonge

Het Nederlandse koningshuis by Arnout van Cruyningen

Juliana by Jolande Withuis

Juliana en Bernhard by Cees Fasseur

Koning Willem III by Dik van der Meulen

Lonely but not alone by Princess Wilhelmina of the Netherlands

Sophie in Weimar by Thera Coppens

Van Loon: Popular Historian, Journalist, and FDR Confidant by
Cornelis Van Minnen

Vorstelijk begraven en gedenken. Funeraire geschiedenis van het
huis Oranje-Nassau by Cees van Raak

Wilhelmina, de jonge Koningin by Cees Fasseur

Wilhelmina, Krijgshaftig in een vormeloze jas by Cees Fasseur

Printed in Great Britain
by Amazon